YOUNG WRITERS
Spellbound

Co Durham

Edited by Jenny Edwards

First published in Great Britain in 1998 by
POETRY NOW YOUNG WRITERS
1-2 Wainman Road, Woodston,
Peterborough, PE2 7BU
Telephone (01733) 230748

All Rights Reserved

Copyright Contributors 1998

HB ISBN 1 86188 833 3
SB ISBN 1 86188 838 4

FOREWORD

In this, our 5th competition year, we are proud to present *Spellbound Co Durham*. This anthology represents the very best endeavours of the children from this region.

The standard of entries was high, which made the task of editing a difficult one, but nonetheless enjoyable. The variety of subject matter, creativity and imagination never ceases to amaze and is indeed an inspiration to us all.

This year's competition attracted the highest entry ever - over 46,000 from all over the UK, and for the first time included entries from English speaking children living abroad.

Congratulations to all the writers published in *Spellbound Co Durham*. We hope you enjoy reading the poems and that your success will inspire you to continue writing in the future.

CONTENTS

Carmel School

Claire Kilgour	1
Lianne Savage	1
Lydia Mangle	2
Katherine Johnsone	2
Laura Joyeux	3
Leanne Wigham	4
Tom Devin	4
Stephanie Thompson	5
Victoria Shaw	6
Richard Gill	6
Jennifer Mary Wiper	7
Daniel Kelly	8
Danielle Miller	9
Katherine Bracken	10
Hannah Davies	11
Jessica Fenwick	11
Nick Lyons	12
Eleanor Firth	13
Paul Trenholme	13

Fyndoune Community College

Martin Jameson	14
Claire Pomphrett	15
Carly Richardson	16
Sarah Wilson	17
Charis Webster	18
Emily Park	18
David Wile	19
Michael Park	20
Gary McDermott	20
Simon Rowell	21
Joanne Waugh	22
Emma Dixon	23
Laura Menzies	24
Katie Petch	25

Andrea Oughton	26
Sarah-Jane Anderson	26
Anna Maria Murray	27
Claire Rossi	28
Kevin Evans	29
Kirsty Stephenson	30
Helen Walters	30
Katy Coles	31
Hayley Finch	32
Andrew Dixon	32
Andrea Youll	33
Sam Hutchinson	33
Kieran Loan	34
Mark Smith	34
Emma Stone	35
Adam English	36
Heather Duncan	36
Lindsay Pearson	37
Sara Winter	38
Rachel Elliott	38
Rachel Walters	39
Alex Huntley	40
Christine Turner	41
Andrew Berry	42
Thoren Webster	42
Colin Reay	43
Claire Bennett	44
Laura McAdams	44
Christopher Calland	45
Dale Farnworth	45
Sumeet Sandhu	46
Aimee Comby	46
Adam Craik	47
Jessica Hinsley	48
Ben Brown	48
Ross Christian	49
Stacey Wood	50
Greg Coates	50

Nicola Thomas	51
Christopher White	51
Kerri Lowden	52
Ruth Maddison	53
Amy Watson	54

Hurworth School

Sarah Welch	54
Lisa Woods	55
Katie Purvis	56
Kate Duffy	56
Michael Gowling	57
Colin Henry	58
Sarah McNulty	58
Lauren Drysdale	59
Andrew Jones	60
Claire Hugill	60
Laura Bright	61
Lloyd Bishop	62
Victoria Chisholm	62
Nicola Foster	63
Sarah-Jane Brown	64
Laura Bernstone	64
Alice Smith	65
Daniel McDowell	66
Philip Masters	67
Emma Todd	68
Rosalyn Smith	69
Laura Chapman	70
Amy Sedgwick	70
Chris Devlin	71
Adam Wilkinson	72
Pippa Baker	73
Steven Jamieson	73
Gemma Lonsdale	74
David Ellis	74
Jane Brazier	75
Samantha Cooper	76

Victoria Paver	77
Kayleigh Evans	78
Lucy Todd	79
Jennifer Sanderson	80
Emma Paver	81
Heather Minto	82
Kelly Pybus	82
Gemma Roberts	83
David Gowling	83
Samantha Young	84
Paul Brentley	84
Katie Hayllar	85
Laura Ward	85
Toni Leach	86
Ben Chapel	86
Peter Hedley	87
Laura Todd	88
Vicki Richards	89
Richard Carlin	89
Michael Chapman	90
Daniel Cooper	90
Jennie Haines	91
Holly Avery	91
Stephanie Hiley	92
John Ilee	92
Victoria McKone	93
Rachael Evans	94
Rachel Hastie	94
Rachel Lambert	95
Lisa McCready	95
Steven Wilson	96
Lyndsey Shaw	97
Vickie Wetherill	97
Mike Brazier	98
Mark Swanwick	98
Daniel Haggart	99
Patricia Machin	100
Claire Fletcher	101

Jane Sutcliffe	102
Suzanne Carter	102
Kevin Smith	103
Catherine Bennison	104
Ben Robertson	104
Louise Roxby	105
Liam Robertson	105
Christina Fossheim	106
David Ralph	106
Tim Covell	107
Rachael Pitt	107
Heidi Fleary	108
Emma Lowrie	108
Mark Flood	109
Krystle Shields	110
Jenna Taylor	110
Craig Buckley	111
Nichola Harkness	112
John Sunter	112
Lee Marsh	113
Helen Easby	113
Kathryn Williams	114
Manuela Hairsine	114

Moorside Comprehensive School

Rachael Herdman	115
Greg Roe	115
Stacy Green	116
Steven Eccles	116
Simon Scarr	117
Kirsty Grant	118
Mandy Davison	118
Craig Suddick	119
Kim Kirsopp	120
Lindsey Gibson	120
Stephanie Graham	121
Rebecca Lister	122
Gina Brewis	122

Jemma Green	123
Victoria Clews	123
Katie Brewis	124
Craig Rogerson	124
Calvin Todd	125
Helen Alderson	126
Kerry Mordue	127
Emma Dawson	128
Stephen Westgarth	129
Michelle Donaghy	130
Amy Matthews	132
Wayne Galloway	133
Jenna Ashton	134
Freya Claydon	135
John Milburn	135
Laura Farthing	136
David Grix	137
Abbie Whitehead	137
Louise Roe	138
Adam Nash	139
Vicky Nash	140

St Bede's School

Jon McClaren	140
Ben Elliott	141
Michelle McMahon	141
Craig Davies	142
Katy McGeary	142
Tracey Dixon	143
Richard Peacock	144
Stuart W Murray	145
Steven Graham	146

St John's School

Paul Walker	146
Michael Hartmann	147
Richard Morley	148
Adam Blenkinsop	149

Jake Farrell	150
Carl McGregor	151
Sarah McGough	152
Victoria Ratcliffe	153
Gemma Bell	154
Richard Simpson	155
Katie Fowler	156
Sara Elmes	157
Hannah Daltry	158
Penny Foster	159
Sean Kay	160
James Davy	160
Sonny Rockett	161
Emma Barker	162
Casey Mangles	163
Philip J Santana Smith	164
Robert Jones	165

St Leonard's RC Comprehensive School

Christopher Ranson	166
Sarah McCully	166
Michael Weetman	167
Adam Sinclair	167
Jennifer Hastings	168
Joanna Jones	168
Peter Burlinson	169
Catherine McKenna	170
Fiona Granlund	170
Adelle Outhwaite	171
Peter Nichols	172
Abigail Duggan	172
Gemma Hewitt	173
Katy Moore	173
Simon Farthing	174
Katrina Hesketh	175
Ian Wilson	176
Kelly Hewitt	176
Philip Curry	177

Katherine Rooke	178
Caroline Marsh	179
Sarah Williams	180
Philip Belton	181
Helen Campbell	181
Laura Young	182
Lydia Davison	182
Helen Jones	183
Sarah Oliver	184
Cheryl Wright	184
Laura O'Hagan	185
Paul Brady	186
Rebecca Roche-Smith	187
Jonathan McIntosh	187
Lucy Glover	188
Catherine Hughes	188
Joy Hewitson	189
Daniel Van Leempoel	190
Samantha Sheen	191
Stephanie Nicholson	191
Marie-Claire Coxon	192
Ian Mullany	193
Christopher Dodds	193
Tony Hutchinson	194
James Hicken	194
Sarah Bailey	195
Cheryl Murphy	196
Natalie Wildish	197
Jonathan Stevenson	198
Emma Hann	198
Lisa Richardson	199
Helena Jackson	200
Jessica Eddie	201
Lianne Crosby	202
James Mallen	202
Robert Paton	203
Ruth Elder	204
Clare Puddifoot	205

Katy Jennings	206
Tom Marley	206
Annalise Simpson	207
Marie Ford	208
Ellena Plumb	208
Rachel Chadwick	209
Elizabeth Powell	209
Rachel Hooper	210
Sean Morris	210
Richard Lyons	211
Eleanor Byrne	211
Kim Coates	212
Jill Richardson	212
Paul Edis	213
Steven Howe	213
Warren Kennick	214
Stacey Denton	214
Philip Morris	215
Claire Gray	216
Daniel McCaffery	216
Richard Villis	217
Chris Brady	218
Sarah Wigham	218
Nicola Goodburn	219
Mark Fleming	220
Jade Mackie	221
Emma Ward	222
Kieran Brookes	223
Sarah-Jane Mason	224
Andrew Murray	225
Vicki Howard	225
Charlotte Kerr	226
Geoffrey Burgess	227
Shelley Griffin	228
Adam Nicholson	228
Peter Hewitt	229
Cora Hanson	230
Emma Kitching	231

Laura Smith	232
Sarah Villis	232
Andrea Muers	233
Helen Timothy	234
Verity Williams	234
Catriona Long	235
Helen Sharp	236
Andrew Steel	236
Emily Dott	237
Aileen Dennis	238
Helen Burnip	239
Joanne Walls	240
Natasha Van Leempoel	241
Stephen Grace	242
Philip Magowan	243
Gavin Bainbridge	244
Kenneth Fox	244
Catie Durbridge	245
Kate Hopgood	246
Rebecca Armstrong	247
Amy Corrigan	248
Elizabeth Finn	249
Jonathan Kitching	250
Jill Mulcahy	250
Grace Potter	251
Emma Hutton	252
Peter Rodriguez	252
Nicola Siberry	253
Laura Edwards	254
Mark Henderson	255
Christopher Veitch	255
Emma Liddle	256
Robert Garside	256
Daryl Hodgson	257
Daniel Bell	257
James Lonergan	258

Shotton Hall Comprehensive School
Sharon Price	258
Danielle Coils	259
Cherrelle Docherty	259
Gill McGowan	260
Kevin Swann	261
Michelle Lacey	261
Samantha Hutchinson	262
Deonne Heatlie	262
Jennifer Collins	263
Christopher Mooney	264
Paul Docherty	264
Amanda Rain	265
Jan Tinkler	265
Gareth Edwards	266
Colin Flatt	266
Deborah Watson	267
Kayleigh Slater	267
David Iley	268
Helen Haley	268
Karl Gippert	269
Lauren Blower	270
Victoria Kate Young	270
Alex Masshedar	271
Graeme Clark	272
Michael Laws	272
Tracy Dodds	273
Barry Carney	274
Kelly Love	275
Daniel Donbauand	276
Stephanie Bailey	276
Bethany Ainsley	277
Andrew Alexander	278
Matthew Foxton	278
Ian Bell	279
Laura Laws	280
Jonathan McNay	281
Charlene Price	282

Lyndsey Todd 283

Wolsingham Comprehensive School
Ann Marie Burke 283
Jonathan Binks 284
Gabriella White 284
Shea Scott 285
Sophie Douglas 286
Nick Grayson 287
Jonathan Elliott 288
Louis Tristram 288
Caroline West 289
Daniel Evans 290
Jill Nattrass 290
Emma Coxon 291
Bennath Evea 292
Michael Stott 292
Alice Cleasby 293
Joanne de Muschamp 294
Adam Crampsie 294
Tabitha Willis 295
Daniel Jackson 295
Rosemary Menes 296
Sarah Donaldson 296
Jamie Allinson 297
Catriona Maddocks 298
Lucy Kilgariff 298
Laurie Shepherd 299
Ashleigh Findeisen 300

THE POEMS

AT NIGHT

The moon smiles happy and bright,
The stars shine bright at night.
The owl hoots clear as a bell,
As the water ripples in the wishing well.
The lights close their eyes,
When the children say their bye, byes.
The sun goes right down,
There's not a sound,
Right through the town.
The sky is as dark as coal,
Nobody is around,
Not a soul.

Claire Kilgour (13)
Carmel School

AT NIGHT

The stars winked like a flashing disco light,
The moon was shimmering and shining like
the flame of a candle!
Car headlights shone in the murky dusk,
Trees swaying in the night's silence.
You hear people laughing and dancing as
they return from a party all drunk and disorderly?
You find yourself gazing up to see
a beautiful ocean of moons,
as they orbit around their planet.
One by one, each and every person turns their
lights out,
and the night is left in the peacefulness
of just your gentle breath.

Lianne Savage (14)
Carmel School

BIG FAT TREE

There's a big fat tree in our garden,
He sits all day, every day,
His branches gracefully waving in the breeze
My great, great grandfather planted it, I am told
So I worked out that it must be old.

This tree we've had for oh so long
Its being here, it is not wrong
It's a family symbol from then to now
It's stayed alive so long I don't know how.

I like our tree better than any other trees.
Waving his branches in the breeze
I hope it stays alive forever
In our back garden sitting there
So everyone can see it grow together.

Lydia Mangle (13)
Carmel School

BY THE SEA

By the sea you and me
On a dark night
The moon shines bright
The waves clang, clash and crash against the cliffs.
The cliffs are crooked old men all in a line,
Groaning as they get crushed by the powerful sea.
The wind whistles whilst the fishes swim in the sea.
By the sea you and me.

Katherine Johnsone (14)
Carmel School

A BAD DAY!

I wake up. Oh no! It's eight thirty!
It's started already, I know.
Inside, our boiler is broken,
Outside, the world's covered in snow.

My hair is a mess from the night,
It doesn't seem to want to stay down.
A curse has been put on my head,
I'll never get rid of this frown.

My friends don't give me much support,
They're feeling bluesy too.
The love of my life can't cheer me up,
'Cause he's off with the flu.

I get home all tired and aching
With homework piled miles high.
I need to relax with a cuppa
But I only have time to sigh.

As I struggle to carry on working,
Frustration builds up inside.
Tenseness and anger from the day
Washes over me in a sudden tide.

I can't do my French or mathematics.
Either one's hard on their own.
I can't write this poem for English,
So get lost, and

Leave me alone!

Laura Joyeux (13)
Carmel School

MY POEM

Cats miaowing
Dogs barking
Crowds at a football game when Newcastle are playing
Crash of the waves against the rocks
Peace and quiet
The songs of birds in the morning
Music on TV.
The footsteps of young children
Children outside laughing
And the jingle of money
The laughter of people on TV
The sound of people enjoying themselves
The crying of newborn babies
The silence of an empty house
The silence in a classroom
The sound of babies playing with toys
The sound of owls howling
And the sound of bones knocking together.

Leanne Wigham
Carmel School

THE PIT LANE

The car purred into the pit lane and came to a halt
The pit crew went into action,
Timing was crucial,
No mistakes must be made.

The jacks popped up into place,
Wheels wrenched off.
Time was passing,
Menu was looking anxious.

Click, and the petrol nozzle was in,
Seconds were ticking by.
Fresh wheels were screwed on,
The petrol nozzle was released, the team stood back.

Menu accelerated hard,
The tyres squealed as the car went back into the race
Black rubber marked the pit lane,
Great stop by Alan Menu at 10.5 seconds.

Tom Devin (13)
Carmel School

WINTER

The snow is falling from the sky
The icicles hang from the window-sill
The children rush to play outside
The adults hide from the winter chill

Building a snowman on the lawn
Sledging swiftly down the bank
Snowballs slicing through the air
Like shells firing from a tank.

Crunching the ice as they march along.
Children are soldiers in a war
Injuries occur but they still battle on
Fighting until they can fight no more.

The snowman is standing, feeling sad
His nose has slipped down on his cheek
His body is slowly beginning to melt
He will be gone by the end of next week.

Stephanie Thompson (13)
Carmel School

THE NIGHT

The night is waiting, wanting, watching you,
so you'd all better run,
keep running until your legs can't carry you,
keep running until you see the sun,
until it captures all your fears,
but watch out night is coming near,
closer, coming, keep on running the night is catching you.
It's like a werewolf wanting its prey,
so you'd all better pray and hope tomorrow is a great day,
and please don't think about your fears,
for the night is quite so near.
It is a great big grisly bear,
waiting for the night to appear,
the night it will kill all that stands before it,
so please stay in bed and don't look for it.

Victoria Shaw (13)
Carmel School

THE TREE

Most days I walk past a tree which seems to be
Staring, staring at me,
It looks at me closely with wood-covered eyes,
Staring at me as I pass it by.

It's been there for ages my grandpa said to me,
As we were walking past that big woody tree,
It groans with the wind and the rain and the snow,
And I always wonder how big it will grow.

It sees me at morning, it sees me at night,
That tree that keeps on watching me pass
By, day and night.
Then one day during autumn the tree was not there,
Gone from the place where it used to stare,
I miss the old tree now that it's gone,
I'm missing the things it's done for so long.

Richard Gill (13)
Carmel School

MY FIRST DAY AT SCHOOL

I approached the school gates feeling nervous and scared.
Buses were coming in and out I had no idea where to go or what to do.
Teachers were running around gathering their forms together.
We gathered in the assembly hall, the air was tense while nervous children reluctantly took their seats.
The head of year 7 made a welcoming speech and the rest of the time the headmaster spoke.
We were whisked off to our form rooms to get sorted out.
When the lunch bell finally rang I headed towards the canteen to find year 7s lining up to get their lunch it was nice (unlike most school dinners).
Lessons! Our form tutor told us all about our lessons and of course the dreaded detention and *homework!*
At precisely 3.35 the bell rang to mark the end of a hectic day (but I enjoyed it) now the best part of the day
Home time!

Jennifer Mary Wiper (11)
Carmel School

First Day At Secondary School

On the way to school,
So nervous.
Have I brought everything, I kept wondering and wondering.
I felt sick. My stomach felt like it was bungee-jumping
from my rib cage. My bag was like an anvil. My heart felt like
                                                                               lump of lead
A zillion thoughts flew round my head like cars on a motorway.
Everything stopped when I saw a group of boys in uniform.
I sighed and my hot breath dissolved in the cold crisp air.
I plodded towards the huge building that towered over me.
The windows were like staring black eyes. The fences were like sharp, metal, pointed teeth. The doors were like gaping mouths ready to swallow you until half-past three.

In school,
so scared.
Big rooms, big corridors, big teachers, big boys and girls.
Big everything!
A thought suddenly exploded into my head.
I'm lost. I must be.
I spotted my form in a room. I opened the creaky door.
Dozens of eyes looked at me, as if I'd committed a crime.
Had I?

I sat down and pulled out my books.
Will I make it through today, I thought.

Going home,
So happy.
I'm glad that's over, I kept sighing and sighing,
I felt well. My stomach felt like it was resting
in my rib cage. My bag was like a feather, my heart
was like a foam cube.
My head was calm, but wait!
What about tomorrow? What if I make a mistake when I work?
What if I . . .

Daniel Kelly (11)
Carmel School

THE NIGHT SKY

At night when the moon begins to show,
like a headlight in the inky blue sky.
The cool autumn breeze swirls and swishes,
the crisp, falling leaves.
A lonesome man out walking his dog,
like a predator in the quiet and peacefulness.

Now the moon is high and the sky is a witch's cloak,
it spreads to keep out the light.
The shadows of fingers scratching at the window pane,
keeps me tucked safely in my bed.
Till slowly my eyes droop,
to take me to a world of dreams.
Now it is getting light,
but the sun does not shine as winter begins to set in.

I see the trees twirling and swaying,
and realise they're not fingers at all.
Now I'm like a soldier preparing to get through another day,
and slowly droplets of rain plip and plop to the ground.

Danielle Miller (14)
Carmel School

My First Day At School

It's my first day at school, after six glorious weeks doing nothing, I have to go back to school.
Tens of billions of thoughts were going round my head:
'Will I get lost?'
'What about the showers in PE?'
'Will I be bullied?'
'Will I get detention?'
Calm down I told myself.
'Katherine are you ready to go now?' shouted my mam.
Go? Go?
All the thoughts came back.
The journey there was the longest journey of my life.
When I got there, I was white!
'Bye pet, enjoy your day,' called mam.
Enjoy my day.
What was she, crazy?
I walked to the form room with my head in the clouds.
Thankfully my form tutor is really nice.
As I walked to my first lesson, I thought I was going to die!
Luckily, it wasn't so bad.
After that lesson, it was break.
Break - aaah! peace and fresh air.
RRRrrrinng - Help, the bell!
Another lesson - science, not my favourite lesson.
Lunchtime!
As quick as lunch came, it was over.
My next lesson was maths - that's OK.
Addition and subtraction drifted through my head.
Rrring - I jumped out of my day-dream.
Next lesson - geography - not too bad
It was hot and sticky in there, then - Rrring!
'How was your day?'
'I *love* it!'

Katherine Bracken (11)
Carmel School

MY NEW SCHOOL

I walk to school with all my friends
We're as terrified as can be,
We try to sound heroic though, it doesn't scare me.
But deep inside our little minds, we're all thinking the same thought,
I wonder what new subjects we will be taught
We arrive at the school gates, and then we wander in,
We try to talk but it's too hard because of the din.
We made our way to the main hall, and I was seated on the chair,
Then all our thoughts and worries we were encouraged to share.
I was made to follow a man I know I've seen before,
Oh yes, I remember, it was on the school tour.
Crowds and crowds of faces all in 7A,
They are all scared as well, what a scary day
At the end of one lesson you're run off your feet,
And it seems like a year before you get to eat!
But I did enjoy my first day, and there's only one rule,
The best place in the world is
                Carmel School!

Hannah Davies (11)
Carmel School

BY THE SEA

The waves jump at the cliffs
like a dog at his master's feet
The seagulls circle round the sands
waiting for crumbs to fall
The sea is deep and dark
like a never ending pit
It tosses boats like corks
in a pan of boiling water
Spinning them like a whirlpool.

Jessica Fenwick (13)
Carmel School

MY FIRST DAY OF SCHOOL

As I walk through the gates
I hear the chant in my mind.
Blazer boy, Blazer boy!
As I walk to the main doors,
there's a sigh of relief
three of my friends are there.

As I look at my watch
the time is 8.45
as I look to admire the grounds
all my friends in a group
come walking up the path
I am not scared anymore
I am not lonely anymore.

As the bell goes we go inside
meet our new teacher
now we get down to work,
not soon after the bell goes, it's break
all the tall people are around me
and I'm squashed.

At lunch break it is the same,
but I broke free
and I walked around with
my new friends
at my new school.

As the day went on
I felt happier and happier
but then the word 'homework'
was mentioned.

Nick Lyons (11)
Carmel School

THE SEA

The sinister sea swishes in and out,
dumping shells and depositing seaweed
Slowly and slyly scraping at the cliff face.
The cliff seems angry,
The sea gurgles with glee, as it devours more and
more of the rugged rock.
A cool wind blows in off the sea, bringing a bitter,
sweet, salty smell
Old as the sea itself.
I gulp up the smell through my nose and mouth
like a fish out of water, or an out of breath runner.
I like the sea, with its turbulent waters, its
unique smell, its lively personality and playful ways.
The sea, a feast for the senses.

Eleanor Firth (13)
Carmel School

THE FOREST IN AUTUMN

Impatient breezes whispering through the trees,
Towering high with knobbly knees.
Autumn leaves tumble to the ground,
Happily twirling and whirling around.
The shimmering stream chatters away,
Serving the thirsty animals every day.
Plants sprouting up from the forest floor,
Each year growing more and more.
Creatures scurrying to and fro,
Preparing themselves for the winter's snow.
The birds are travelling south again,
Just in time for the winter to set in.

Paul Trenholme (14)
Carmel School

SPELL TO MAKE LITTLE BROTHERS DISAPPEAR

Jump around the cauldron there,
Placing in some bat wing hair.

Toad's eye
Newt's tongue
Bat's wing
Goat's lung.

Dead man's blood in it goes,
And after that the dragon's nose.

Toad's eye
Newt's tongue
Bat's wing
Goat's lung.

Skin of frog bubbling away,
Add the bills we didn't pay.

Toad's eye
Newt's tongue
Bat's wing
Goat's lung.

Cheddar cheese, very smelly
Now a horse's dappled belly.

Toad's eye
Newt's tongue
Bat's wing
Goat's lung.

Finally we have our potion
For our most evil notion.

Toad's eye
Newt's tongue
Bat's wing
Goat's lung.

Now my brother disappears
Once I add the panda's ears.

Vamoose!

(Quietly in a whisper)
Toad's eye
Newt's tongue
Bat's wing
Goat's lung.

Martin Jameson (11)
Fyndoune Community College

WITCHES' FUN

I can't wait for the spell to be done
Making it I've had lots of fun,
In there are all my favourites.
Boy called Simon, girl called Mavis.
Hand of black peas
Polka dots,
Add some wood off a baby's cot,
Rattle snake's rattle
Glow bug's glow,
Oh this will be quite a show.
Into the bowls,
Onto the plate
Or should I serve it on a slate.

Cackle, cackle, laughing with glee,
Adding the sting of a deadly bee,
Cackle, cackle, laughing with glee,
I'll tell you now, don't mess with me!

Claire Pomphrett (12)
Fyndoune Community College

SPELL TO BRING A LITTLE JOY!

To bring a smile,
Add the joy of rabbits playing in the meadows,
The smell of flowers on a sunny day.

Stir well to mix the joy
And soon the world will be full of smiles.

Add a touch of money
Making poverty a thing of the past.
Make criminals leave the world behind.

Stir well to mix the joy
And soon the world will be full of smiles.

Make each summertime beautifully hot,
Add a lot of Christmases and snow.
Don't forget the chocolate!

Stir well to mix the joy
And soon the world will be full of smiles.

Add the happiness that birthdays bring,
Sprinkle in the magic world of fantasy
And stars that twinkle in the night.

Stir well to mix the joy
And soon the world will be full of smiles.

With a wave of my wand
And my powerful chant
Let the world be a happy fairy tale.

Carly Richardson (11)
Fyndoune Community College

THERE SHE SAT...

There she sat, dark and grim
Her pointy hat with a thick rim
There's a spider hanging from the wall
I heard a bat's high-pitched call
Her shelves were filled with bottles and jars
I read the labels here they are:-

Frogs' legs, wooden pegs
Sheep's eye, brain pie
I felt sick but I'd only read four
Something forced me to read some more
Old boot leather, stormy weather
Giant nits, a thousand zits

That was it I couldn't go on
Then I heard her chanting a song
She chanted the names that I had just read
She straightened up and I saw her head
Her nose was crooked pointy and long
Still she continued to chant her song.

She moved to the window and looked out
She threw back her head and I heard her shout
'I'm going now but I'll be back.'
She jumped out and I heard a crack
I listened hard and heard a moan
I waited for silence then she was gone.

Sarah Wilson (12)
Fyndoune Community College

SPELL TO GET RID OF MY BROTHER

Frogs' legs,
Mouldy eggs,
A wasp's sting,
The eye of a king.

Stir it with a twig and make it really big.

A rabbit's ear,
The head of a deer,
Dirty muck,
The bill of a duck.

Stir it with a twig and make it really big.

Sharp glass,
New, green grass,
Toenail of a bear,
Witches' hair.

Stir it with a twig and make it really big.

Purple and pink
Poisonous ink.

Stir it with a twig and make it really big!

Charis Webster (11)
Fyndoune Community College

A SMILE SPELL

Chocolate, ice-cream, yellow and red.
Come and make me smile.

Sunshine, birthdays, Christmas trees.
Come and make me smile.

Money, presents, holidays.
Come and make me smile.

Thunder, lightning, rain, rain, rain.
Come and make me smile.

New clothes, shopping, going out.
Come and make me smile.

No school, homework, just 3.15.
Come and make me smile

Emily Park (11)
Fyndoune Community College

SPELL TO TAKE OVER THE WORLD

Take the tip from a dart
And a human's heart.
Add poison from a frog
And a paw from a dead dog.

If it doesn't hurt add
Just a little dirt.

Lungs of panda
Ears of Granada.

Pour a pint of boiling blood
Stop everyone from being good.

Drop in a snail's shell
And all the things from hell.

Cut it with a knife
Bringing evil back to life!

David Wile (11)
Fyndoune Community College

A Spell To Bring A Smile

Chocolate fudge and cherry sauce
this should bring a smile.

Izzy whizzy, let's get busy.
Bring a smile to every face.

Favourite bikes
and little tikes that run round and play.

Izzy whizzy, let's get busy.
Bring a smile to every face.

Favourite films
and their stars

Izzy whizzy, let's get busy.
Bring a smile to every face.

Mars bars and Snickers
liquorice and gum.

Michael Park (12)
Fyndoune Community College

Snow Spell

Come down snow
Snow come down.

Fall on the earth
Like a blanket of light.

White and bright
Sledging tonight!

Turning the corner
Fast as I go,
Quicker and quicker
Until it is night.

Come down snow
Snow come down.

Gary McDermott (11)
Fyndoune Community College

THE FALL OF THE WITCH

Frogs' legs are burned and all over the floor,
The cauldron is cold now and the mixture solid,
Broken glass of a jar is stuck in the cat's side like a rock on a smooth landscape
The cat's blood flows like a river to the floor where an army of rats drink it as if it was water.
The darkness of the boarded-up room concealed the ugly features of the witch's rotting old body.
She died a painful death according to the terrible open white mouth,
She is dressed in a black robe which hides a skinny cold body,
the half-dead bat drags itself across the hearth only to fall to its death into the cinders of the fire,
A battered broom is propped up in the corner, next to where a policeman now stood.
The smell was horrific,
The policeman turned and ran,
Screaming like a helpless baby,
The witch has left.
She rests in peace forever.

Simon Rowell (12)
Fyndoune Community College

THE WITCH DOWN OUR STREET

She has no big warts,
And has no black hat,
She isn't old and wrinkled,
And has no black cat.

She wears dark black clothes,
Which are raggy and torn,
Her skin's white as snow,
Her shoes are all worn.

The small children fear her,
Her eyes are cold and dark,
She comes out when the sun's set,
And walks in the park.

She lives in a house,
At the end of our street,
All spooky and gloomy,
No one dares trick or treat!

The spells that she casts,
The broth that does bubble,
We daren't take a peek,
We'd be in deep trouble.

Her hair black as ebony,
Her fingers long and thin,
She'll coldly stare at you,
She's so full of sin.

I pray you'll never meet her,
The witch down our street,
That she'll leave you alone,
If you act innocent and sweet.

So you have been warned,
You can't run, you can't hide,
This time tomorrow,
You could be deep fat fried!

Joanne Waugh (14)
Fyndoune Community College

A Spell To Bring A Smile

To bring a smile
Just wait a while,
Then when it's time
Ring a chime.
Chant into the pot
'Smile, smile.'
Make it up
So that the world's a happy lot.

Add to the pot
Lots and lots of sweets.
Then clap a steady beat
And chant into the pot
'Smile, smile.'
Make it up
So that the world's a happy lot.

Whisper a magic word.
Clean up the world's dirt.
And chant into the pot
'Smile, smile.'
Make it up
And now the world's a happy lot.

Emma Dixon (11)
Fyndoune Community College

A WELL-KNOWN WITCH

She's a very old lady,
With warts on her face,
She can disappear,
Without a trace.

She wears black clothes,
All old and tatty,
She smells so bad,
And looks so scratty.

She has a black cat,
All skin and bones,
As it walked down the corridor,
All you heard were moans.

She is very small,
And quite plump,
One arm was long,
The other a stump.

Being so fat,
She's not very quick,
Apart from when,
She's on her broomstick.

She has witchcraft in her cupboard
Spell books on her shelves,
She has no friends at all,
Not even goblins or elves.

Some say she's evil
Some say she's mad,
Whichever is true,
It's all very sad.

But she's still a witch,
No matter what!

Laura Menzies (13)
Fyndoune Community College

WHAT ARE WITCHES?

Where do all the witches stay?
Is it near or far away?
Do they just come out at night
So they can give people a fright?

Do all witches have warts
And tall black hats?
Do they turn people into frogs?
Or take care of lost dogs?

Maybe witches aren't that bad
Or I might be wrong and they are all raving mad.
Do witches really exist?
Or are they just a made up fairytale
Left behind in the mist?

Katie Petch (13)
Fyndoune Community College

THE WITCH

Eye of a newt,
Leg of a frog,
Tail of a lizard,
That lived in a log,
Mix them, mix them,
Add a little sick,
Cream it, cream it,
Till it's nice and thick,
Blood of a rat,
Teeth of a cat,
Mix altogether,
And put it in the oven,
When it's ready eat at once,
It's better when it's hot.

Andrea Oughton (12)
Fyndoune Community College

SPELL TO MAKE SNOW

Snow!
Come down thick
Heavy on the land.

I want to swim in the snow
Like fish swim in the sea.

I want to roll down the snow
Like a ball rolls down the hill.

Snow!
Come down thick
Heavy on the land.

Sarah-Jane Anderson (12)
Fyndoune Community College

HALLOWE'EN

Tonight's the night that witches fly,
Whizzing in the cloudy sky.
It's cold and dark,
I can hear the witches' lark.

On the shelf a bottle or two,
Of very smelly gooey stew.
Out the witches tell,
Their new and evil spell.

Zip, zap, zipidy, zip
Pip, pop, pipidy, pip
Dip, dap, dipidy, dip
Zip, zap, zipidy, zip.

Ha ha ha! In it goes,
Smelly, hairy, human toes.
Tee hee hee! Cackle in glee,
In goes one bottle of dog wee.

Add one pinky pig,
A very spicy fig.
A pig's trotter
The bubbles get hotter.
Zip, zap, zipidy, zip
Turn this dog into a log.
Turn this frog into a dog.
Zip, zap, zipidy, zap.

Anna Maria Murray (13)
Fyndoune Community College

SPELLBOUND

Bound by a spell,
Those witches did it well,
Can't find an antidote,
Tried eating the eye of toad.
Killed the cat,
Ate its fat.
Fleeced the sheep,
Ate its underneath.
Ate a girl,
My head's in a whirl.
I'm no nearer to being free.

Bound by a spell,
Those witches did it well,
Can't find an antidote,
For the witches' deadly cloak.
Wandering around,
No answer is found.
I'll cover my head,
I'll soon be dead.
I'm not going to die,
For now I know why.
Now I'm nearly free.

Bound by a spell,
Those witches did it well,
Not well enough,
For now I'm out of the cuffs.
I'm running around,
I'm kissing the ground.
I'm praising the sky,
For what I don't know why.
Now I'm going for revenge,
I'm going to perform the greatest avenge.
Those witches will be dead,
'Cause I'll chop off their heads.

Claire Rossi (12)
Fyndoune Community College

WITCHES!

With a pointed hat.
And a crooked nose.
A big black cat,
And black baggy clothes.
She has warts on her hands.
And warts on her fingers.
Musty smells and
Magic lingers.
She stirs the cauldron
With a big black stick
Making sure
That it's not too thick.

Kevin Evans (12)
Fyndoune Community College

SPELLBOUND

Miss Kenvil lives at number 13,
Unlucky for some but not witches,
The kids on the block are so frightened of her.
Rumour has it they saw her flying on a broom,
Shouting stuff like,
                'Bubble, bubble,
                  Toil and trouble.'
Her house is black and dull,
    like the midnight sky,
The moon glitters on her house, like diamonds.
But no one dares look over the fence to see her in the yard.
At night the chimney smokes, like a cauldron would.
But no one will ever know now she's moved away.

Kirsty Stephenson (12)
Fyndoune Community College

THE TEACHER WITCH

She scowls, she laughs.
She is our teacher
disguised in women's clothes.
She is the evillest of women the world has ever seen.
Wearing all black over her slender body with
shining silver jewellery.
Her face, a perfect white and her lips a fresh blood red.
Her black spring-like curls drowning her face.
With a blood-curdling laugh that floods the halls.
With long jugular-piercing nails to match her lips.
The children are silent for they are petrified of the evil witch.

Helen Walters (12)
Fyndoune Community College

The Last Dragon

The last dragon lay in his cave all alone.
His ribs heaved as he breathed
He let out a sigh of despair.
It's not fair it's too cold as his breath hit the air.
'My fire's gone out,' he said with a shout.
But no one could hear
Because he was the last dragon.

Suddenly to his surprise a stranger stood before him.
'What's this?' he said to the beast
'I am the last dragon on earth and I can't even hiccup a spark,'
'Fear not,' said the man for I have the answer
I am a wizard you see and as old as the Ark.'

He put down his sack on the cold damp floor.
And reached right inside it and pulled out a door
'Go through the door' he said to the beast 'and on the other side
your mind will be at peace.'
The dragon stood up and just like magic he entered a world
that made his sadness cease.

Before him lay a world full of joy
Dragons everywhere oh how his heart soared
Fire shot from his mouth as he let out a great roar
He wasn't the last dragon on earth anymore.

Katy Coles (11)
Fyndoune Community College

Witch's Stew

Eye of a newt, leg of a toad, head of a bat,
arm of a rat,
Throw them all in that bubbling cauldron,
With a pinch of pepper and mix it around.
Add the salt till it starts to bubble.
Ear of frog, tooth of a rabbit, claw of a dog, some
fur from a cat.
Mix them all together, watch it bubble
and wait till it starts firing at you.
Put into jars then get on your broom
and fly into the night.
Spread the magic potion around.
Watch all the children fall right into your hands.

Hayley Finch (12)
Fyndoune Community College

Spellbound

Eye of newt, next door's cat,
five frogs' legs, a wing of bat.
A foot of rabbit just for luck,
have another look at the spell book.
A smelly sock, five old toads,
a dead man's finger, a broken bone.
Stir it, stir it, serve it up,
and watch it as it bubbles up.
Eyes pop out, and arms drop out,
legs fall off, and feet drop off.
And just for afters, some drop dead
oh what a great potion.

Andrew Dixon (12)
Fyndoune Community College

SPELLBOUND

She sat . . .
rocking in her chair
She sang . . .
singing in her evil voice
No one will talk to her
No one will look at her
They know what she is like.

She got up . . .
Walked over to the window
She stared . . .
Staring with her bright red eyes
No one will talk to her
No one will look at her
For they know she's out for . . .

    The Kill!

Andrea Youll (12)
Fyndoune Community College

THE CRICKETTY CRACKETTY HOUSE

In the cricketty cracketty house
Lived a cricketty cracketty man
The cricketty cracketty man
Had a cricketty cracketty van
In the cricketty cracketty van
There was a cricketty cracketty can.

Sam Hutchinson (11)
Fyndoune Community College

BUBBLE BUBBLE

Bubble bubble let's make trouble

Lizard's tail
Guts of a pig
The blood of an ox
Bubble bubble let's make trouble

The teeth of a rat
The tusks of an elephant
The shell of a tortoise
Bubble bubble let's make trouble

The rattle of a rattlesnake
The wool of a sheep
The beak of a kestrel
Bubble bubble we've made trouble.

Kieran Loan (11)
Fyndoune Community College

UNTITLED

Stuart Pearce is so fierce
Andy Gorham is a showman
Niall Quinn will always win
Alan Shearer gets dearer and dearer
Ian Wright flies like a kite
Ruel Fox looks like a box
Glenn Hoddle is a doddle
David Seamen changes to a demon
Kevin Ball is very tall
Roy Keane is very mean
Richard Ord is very bored.

Mark Smith (12)
Fyndoune Community College

SPELLBOUND

Devil's canyon where he be
Witches, goblins, cats and fleas
The devil sits upon his throne
Waiting while the witches moan

People watch the witch's stew
Round and round the cauldron flew
Goblins watch at witching hour
Mind their might
And watch their power

Devil tastes
He does not like
He says
'What is this
Goo and slime'

The witches watch
She screams and fled
The devil says
'I'm going to bed'

Devil wakes
To screams of fear
The witch has gone
And so's the beer.

Emma Stone (12)
Fyndoune Community College

SPELLBOUND

The witch came from the cave,
So she could have a wave.
When she came to me,
She said 'Would you like to have tea?'
When I got to the cave,
I thought I was very brave.
When it was time for tea,
She said 'Come with me.'
When I saw her cauldron,
I thought there was a problem,
And when she tried to throw me in it,
I ran as fast as a whippet.
Out of the cave and down the hill,
She was after me, ready to kill.
Half way down the hill I saw a wishing well,
Then I decided to make my own spell.
Make this witch disappear,
So nobody else will live in fear.
In a flash of light she was gone from sight
And all the people celebrated that night.

Adam English (12)
Fyndoune Community College

ROCK A BYE BABY

Rock a bye baby,
Your nana's in the Navy,
She sails through the night,
Casting spells left and right,
Rock a bye baby.

Drink a bye baby,
Your eyes glow like crazy,
Nana taught you right,
Here a bite, there a bite!
Drink a bye baby.

Heather Duncan (12)
Fyndoune Community College

UNTITLED

Where can I hide?
Where can I hide?
In a forest so green
Or with a witch so mean.
Where is her cat?
Where is her cat?
It's so silent at night
Like a cat out of sight.
Where will she put me?
Where will she put me?
In a cauldron so hot
Or a big cooking pot.
Where might she eat me?
Where might she eat me?
On her dirty old broom or just
In her living room.
What will she eat me with?
What will she eat me with?
With dead frogs' eyes or
Ten blind flies.

Lindsay Pearson (12)
Fyndoune Community College

SPELLBOUND

As I walked through the streets
On a cold black night,
A woman out of nowhere gave me a fright.
She grabbed my face, her hands were so cold.
How long will I live, will the story be told?
She dragged me away to a cold empty part,
She got out a knife she was ready to start.
She cut off my toes, sliced skin off my back,
What did she do next, I don't know, I've lost track.
As I feel myself rising, the world I'm above,
Flying over the clouds, I feel like a dove.
What else did she do, did she cut off my head?
Oh no, I've reached Heaven, she killed me,
I'm dead!

Sara Winter (13)
Fyndoune Community College

WITCHES' SPELL

W ith evil around her,
I   tching her head,
T witching her nose,
C atching the cat,
H allowe'en is coming again.
E vil eyes passing by,
S limy witches that's what they are.

S limy witches,
P icking their noses.
E vil looking eyes,
L ooking at children,
L aughing to kill.

Rachel Elliott (12)
Fyndoune Community College

The Witch's Spell

She begins to say the words,
Her voice harsh and clear.
The fire crackles in the corner,
The spell is nearly here.

The silence is broken when the clock chimes twelve,
The cat jumps high up into the air,
And opens the window to let in
The cold night air.

She grabs the potion from the chair,
And mounts herself upon her carriage through the air.
The broom takes off and out she goes.

Off she flies through the sky,
Delivering her secret potion.
Her eyes fixed straight ahead,
Glazed in the moonlit sky.

The moon shines down,
Showing her ugly figure.
The world below all asleep,
Unaware of what's above.

She arrives on time,
At the church gate.
Slowly she walks and places the potion by the great door,
Then she runs and off she flies.

The rest is a mystery,
And left for minds to swirl,
Over the mystery of the spell.

Rachel Walters (13)
Fyndoune Community College

I Hadn't a Clue!

I once knew a witch,
We used to go out together,
Shopping and meals,
That type of thing.
Something really puzzled me,
When people saw her,
They'd run and hide,
I didn't know why.

On my birthday,
She took me out for a meal.
She got me these jeans too.
We hardly knew each other.
At the restaurant no one,
No one would serve us,
Or bring us the bill,
I didn't know why.

Last week
She took me to see her house.
It was strange,
All black.
Her oven was a strange shape,
Round.
There were spiders and webs all around,
I'm scared of spiders.

She asked me to take
A closer look at her oven.
I did that all right,
Head first in it.
I think she was uptight,
People were scared of her,
I didn't know why,
I do now, miaow!

Alex Huntley (13)
Fyndoune Community College

THE HORRIBLE DINNER

Tongue of a lizard, a sting of a bee,
An eye of a cow, a tail of a pig.
Mix together with a wave of my stick,
Now I am ready for a nice lovely feast.

Got to have pudding,
What can I have?
Maybe some moles' eyes and a skin of a bat.
Mix together yum yum yum,
Eat it up crumb by crumb.

Very thirsty, what can I have?
Lots of eyeballs, followed by bat.
Take your time and drink it up,
Yum yum I am now full up.

Christine Turner (12)
Fyndoune Community College

Witch's Poem

Her pointy hat a gloomy black,
You can smell the evilness in the air.
The cat sulks in the corner,
The air is bare.
The warty witch starts her spell:
A dash of hair,
An evil eye,
A toad's leg,
A bat's wing,
A little bit of tail.
Give it a stir,
Count to three
And 'wizidi'.

A perfect spell to kill the kids in Spell Town,
The gerbil ready to be tested on,
It's squeaking frantically
But the witch is evil as can be,
So tests it on the gerbil.
The gerbil gave its final squeak and died an instant death,
The witch gave an evil laugh like an elephant in the bath.
Her plan is bound to work,
I hope someone can kill her.

Andrew Berry (12)
Fyndoune Community College

My Social Diary!

A witch at night flying on her broom,
Going very fast passing the moon.

A witch at a fancy dress,
Looking really ugly and a mess.

A witch at holy evening,
Casting, flying, and screaming.

Thoren Webster (12)
Fyndoune Community College

THERE'S A WITCH ON THE PITCH!

I went to watch a football match,
With me mate nicknamed Patch.
In the middle of the game,
When Shearer took his free shot aim,
A witch,
Jumped on the pitch.
'That wasn't a foul,'
As the cat went growl.
'There's no free kick.'
'You lunatic,'
She shouted at the ref.

At that time along came the guard.
She turned around and saw the guard,
Picked up her broom
And said 'Kazoom,'
And out of the stick
Flew a brick,
And knocked the guard right out.

After that the crowd went wild,
The air went mild
And the witch just disappeared.

Colin Reay (13)
Fyndoune Community College

Spellbound

A fairy tale witch
Is a different thing
More like a king.

The ruler of the country
With loads of spells
All dressed in black
Who lives in the dells.

They read in stories
About how she lives
Eating animals wherever she is
Frogs and snails
And cats and dogs
They're all very tasty
Whatever she is.

Claire Bennett (13)
Fyndoune Community College

Spellbound

S cary witches
P icking their noses
E vil eyes all around
L ooking for children
L aughing all night
B opping up and down
O ld looking witches
U gly looking people
N ever to be seen again
D evil things they are.

Laura McAdams (12)
Fyndoune Community College

THE VISIT

They fell from Mars
travelling through the stars.

They came from space
to meet the human race.

Their only concern
is to help us learn.

To live in peace
our guns will all cease.

To live with nature
making the world's new future.

They left through the beam
the people kept their dream.

Christopher Calland (12)
Fyndoune Community College

SPELLBOUND

S pooky
P eople
E at
L aurence's
L olly
B ecause
O f
U nexplained
N aughty
D udes.

Dale Farnworth (12)
Fyndoune Community College

20TH CENTURY WITCH

Imagine a witch from the 20th Century,

What spells would she make?
What stuff would she take?

Would a witch be even meaner? A 20th Century witch?
Would she ride on a vacuum cleaner? A 20th Century witch?
Would she still have a black cat? A 20th Century witch?
She might just have a Virtual Pet! A 20th Century witch!

Would she have warts all over? A 20th Century witch?
She might have had a make over! A 20th Century witch!

Would she use her cauldron? A 20th Century witch?
She might use your mum's cooking pot! A 20th Century witch.

Sumeet Sandhu (11)
Fyndoune Community College

A SPELL TO MAKE MY BROTHER THE BEST FOOTBALLER EVER

A footballer's smelly sock,
Mix some fish up in a wok,
Put it in with the smelly sock.

Bubble, bubble, toil and trouble,

A big boot,
An owl's hoot,
Mix together,

Bubble, bubble, toil and trouble.

Aimee Comby (11)
Fyndoune Community College

DEATH SPELL

Teacher's brain (very rare),
Fish scale, monkey hair,
A cow's eye,
Cheese pie,
Owl wing, ear of hare.

Wheel of car, lions' tails,
A couple of quails,
Porcupine quill,
Then you will,
Need shells from some snails.

You need a few,
Tongues of kinkajou,
A bread crust,
A bucket of rust
And a stick or two.

Take an unpaid bill,
A cupful of dill,
A frog (frisky),
Bottle of whisky,
A horrible tasting pill.

A rock from the sky,
The leg of a fly,
Stomach of whale,
Part of a rail,
Smell this and die.

Adam Craik (12)
Fyndoune Community College

A Spell To Make Your Sister Disappear

Mix well upon this spell
Make the mixture churn
Let the poison burn.

Slime of snail, spike of hog
Horse's head, lice of log.

Cat's ears, dog's nose
Wasp's sting, man's toes.

Blood of sister, foal of bird
Mix an ounce of lemon curd.

Mother's nails, brother's hair
Snake's tongue, one whole bear.

Eggs of fish, teacher's wart
Slime of maggot, hammerhead shark.

As we chant upon this night
So I looked left and right
Take a cat's and mouse's ear
Make my sister disappear.

Jessica Hinsley (11)
Fyndoune Community College

Spellbound Bad And Good

'Hubble, bubble, lots of trouble,'
said the witch casting her spells.
'Make the towns turn into rubble,
Take the water from the village wells.

Hubble, bubble, end all trouble,'
said the good witch with a smile.
'Build the towns up from rubble,
Working happily all the while.'

Ben Brown (11)
Fyndoune Community College

HOW TO MAKE A TEACHER DISAPPEAR

Take a cauldron big enough
to fit all your stuff into it
Take a dog's head
An eye of a cat
An ear of a cow
A heart of a pig
Put it all into the cauldron
Then add more
Put a five-pound note into it
Add a foot of a goat
Horns of a goat
A tail of a fox
but by now it should be ready
Add a pencil
Add a pen
Then add one more thing
A head of your very best thing
Then it should be ready
and be ready for the
      best time of your life.

Ross Christian (11)
Fyndoune Community College

SPELLBOUND

Hubble bubble I smell trouble,
Bubble hubble I smell stew.
Hubble bubble I smell children,
Hubble bubble grab and chew.

Huggle snuggle cauldron trouble,
Snuggle huggle double trouble.
Huggle snuggle Warty's up,
Snuggle huggle the twins are in trouble.

Cats and bats are smelly little rats,
Bats and cats are ugly mats.
Cats and bats are cuddly mats,
Bats and cats are smelly little
        catsss.

Stacey Wood (11)
Fyndoune Community College

SPELLBOUND

Here I sit all alone
Wondering what to put in this poem.
I can't think what to write
On this Wednesday night.
Mam has just brought in my tea
Off to the youth club I must flee.

Greg Coates (11)
Fyndoune Community College

WITCHES

She rides through the night
Shielding out all the light
She rides through roads
Looking for frogs and toads.

She looks for bats
And eyes from rats
Her black cat sits on the hay
Trying to find somewhere to lay.

Her cauldron black
She throws in a sack
She adds some more in
She throws in a sin.

Nicola Thomas (11)
Fyndoune Community College

THE SPELLING TEST

Take a letter from the alphabet
Any letter you like please do.

Maybe better take a few
Add a pen, pencil make that 22.

Add a brain, if not what a shame
But if you don't pass you'll take the blame.

Well at the end the teacher went
Round the bend.

I got an A, yes I did that day.
It worked it did, oh yes it did.

Christopher White (12)
Fyndoune Community College

THE WITCH

She looks normal by day
But not by night
She took off her wig
And gave us a fright

Her fingers were long
Bony and thin
She smelt of the pong
That you get from the bin

She walked to her house
We followed her there
She opened the door
With a stony stare

We ran to the window
Laughing with fear
And were very surprised
With what we did hear

She was chanting away
Cackling with joy
Making a spell
For every girl and boy

The spell that we heard
Made us shiver and shake
It whistled out of the wind
And made our hearts bump and ache

Girls will be boys
And boys will be girls
Girls will have hairy legs
And boys will wear pearls

We scampered away
And she cackled with glee
We know she's a witch
Just look round and see!

Kerri Lowden (13)
Fyndoune Community College

A Witch's Spell!

Hubble bubble big trouble
Fire burn and cauldron bubble.

In the pot a leg of a spider
Burning like a bubble.
A head of a cow and a wing of a bat
A nose of a dog and a leg of a cat.

Hubble bubble big trouble
Fire burn and cauldron bubble.

Bubble bubble lots of trouble
In the pot with lots of bubbles.
The ear of a pig and the leg of an earwig
Burning like a bubble.

Hubble bubble big trouble
Fire burn and cauldron bubble.

Ruth Maddison (11)
Fyndoune Community College

THE WITCH NEXT DOOR

There was an old lady
Who lived in her house.
She never came out
To water her plants.

I saw her once
Down the street.
I don't know what
She was doing digging weeds.

I wish I could explain
I wish I could tell.
But I think my neighbour
Is a *witch!*

Amy Watson (14)
Fyndoune Community College

THE PLACE

The gate holds the entrance to a forbidden place,
Where the buildings are monuments to a forgotten race.
The floorboards sigh with memories of years,
A time when the people had no knowledge of fears.
Eyes peer out from every space,
Everywhere I look I see a haunted face.
People's cries echo around,
Their despair vibrating through the ground.
The Royal flag hangs tattered and torn,
Like the rest of the city it hangs forever forlorn.

Sarah Welch (14)
Hurworth School

SOCCER SENSATIONS

Mr Bailey running about,
He loved football,
There was no doubt.

His purple bottoms
And yellow socks,
He did not like those
Nasty knocks.

He shouted and cheered,
For the ball to be passed,
Never seen him run so fast.

Always bragged about
The goals he scored,
He wouldn't just let
Them be ignored.

Coming to school
With a smile on his face,
Even though Sunderland
Are a disgrace.

He thought the best
Of everyone,
Laughing, joking,
Carrying on.

And now today,
He's up and gone,
Smiling down on everyone.

Lisa Woods (15)
Hurworth School

MY RAT

Some people think my rat's disgusting
Carrying vermin from place to place.
They're scared of his teeth and not trusting
His claws and his long solemn face.

His tail is as long as an earthworm
And with black, beady eyes that may pop.
They don't like the way that he squiggles and squirms
When he tries to jump into your top.

But personally, I think he's excellent
Although most people would disagree.
The only bad thing is his excrement
And my friends have started to see

That it doesn't matter what they say
I still think he's a softy.
No one will ever change my ways
I'll still love my rat, Lofty.

Katie Purvis (14)
Hurworth School

HOLIDAY SUNSET

At first glance it was as beautiful as a butterfly
And as white as snow.
I entered through the large glass door
To see a beautiful sight.

I got our key and the bell boy lead the way
Up the twisting stairway.
From the balcony you could see the sun
Setting over the clear blue sea.

I awoke to see the sun arising
And the sound of children playing in the pool.
I stepped out of bed and looked at the breathtaking
View of white sand, blue sea and palm trees.

The two weeks were nearly over.
The sunset I was watching would be the last,
But this would be the memory I would never forget.
The beautiful sunset.

Kate Duffy (13)
Hurworth School

CITY

City reaching to the sky
City waking from the long night.

People rushing around its buildings
Running in and out its inner workings.
Panes of glass staring round
Watching people on the ground
Making sure they do no wrong.

Traffic weaving through the gaps
Of the buildings hand in hand.

Darkness comes and so do people
Walking round from pubs to clubs
Many people very little clothing.

Music playing through the night
The city does not get much sleep.
But when morning comes
City reaches to the sky
City waking from the long night.

Michael Gowling (15)
Hurworth School

RIVER

River is old and wise
Strong and bold.

River babbles every day
To mother earth
Flowing through her veins.

River watches humans
Kill his mother
Pollute his twin brother.

He is father to water life
But he is killing them
As we are killing him.

The business man has money
In the corner of his eye.
He dumps waste in the river.

We must save river
To save ourselves.

Colin Henry (16)
Hurworth School

THERE STANDS A GHOST

There she stands all in white,
Her silver hair flowing in the dim candle light,
Pale white face, and eyes of gold,
Her hands when you touch them, they're cold,
She'll stand there and stare,
She'll look in despair,
As if to say,
'Does nobody care?'

Sarah McNulty (11)
Hurworth School

SNOW

Snow falling from the sky,
Snow falling in your eye.
On the roof, on the ground,
Falling, falling all around.

You wear your coat,
You wear your hat.
In your coat,
You look so fat.

You melt in the sun,
You lay in the shade.
But in people's minds,
You quickly do fade.

You block the roads,
You stop the traffic.
You make people skid,
You cause havoc.

You are so soft,
You feel so cold.
You come so new,
You go so old.

When you go,
You leave the ground wet.
But when you were here,
We will never forget.

Lauren Drysdale (13)
Hurworth School

Terry

My grandad Terry
has a nose for a bargain,
a ghostly figure
he haunts car boot sales.
Weighed down with carrier bags
he trudges his way home.
'What have you bought now?'
my grandma wails
'Presents.' His eyes glint with the memories of
bargains bought.
Presents purchased.
Treasures,
all of which go into the attic
with . . .
all . . .
the rest . . .

Andrew Jones (14)
Hurworth School

The Sea

The waves roaring,
The waves crashing,
The waves tumbling.
The sea is like a living thing.

Salt water rolling,
Froth and foam raging,
Slapping the golden sand
Like a huge sea serpent thundering around.

It heaves and splutters,
Bashing around
Like a deep blue body,
Becoming angry and demanding.

The sea glimmers azure
With boats on the horizon,
Gradually settling
As the monster begins to sleep.

Claire Hugill (13)
Hurworth School

LONDON

London is a place I go
Every other year or so
With busy roads
And big streets too
What street I'm in I haven't a clue

Look there's the Thames moving as quick as a cheetah
                                     through Hyde Park.
Look there's the Queen parading down Mayfair like a lion,
                                     king of the jungle.

The West End is where the shows begin
With Starlight Express and Les Miserables and more I'm sure.
The crowds turn up for an exciting night
And watch the stars act their fight.

Finally as we conclude our tour
(We can't go to Harrods because we're too poor)
We'll have one last ride around London's streets.
Then off home we'll go all packed and neat.

Laura Bright (13)
Hurworth School

Going To Heaven

A white light shone before me,
As the soul was separated.
Slowly it started to float upon me
As the golden gates greatly separated.

The adventure of life had come to an end,
As the rules of life started to bend
A new life I wish to lend
Because my old life I cannot mend.

A single bang and it was over
As I fell from the white cliffs of Dover.
The rocks with my blood it started to cover
It's too late, it was truly over.

Lloyd Bishop (13)
Hurworth School

Spain

When I arrived it was as silent as a mouse,
The venue was correct so I entered.
From the marble floor to the comfy seat,
I was shown the room I had rented.

I got to the pool side, the crew were there,
The sound of splashing and swishing of the pool below.
The smell of sun-tan lotion filled the air.

At night it was as loud as a zoo,
The sound of drink glasses clattering and voices speaking.
The dancing on the stage and the music too.

Victoria Chisholm (13)
Hurworth School

The South Park

Acres of grass and greenery spread over the park,
Clusters of flourishing woodland, dense, thick and dark.
A lake full of rubbish and brown, murky, polluted water,
It is the cause of the animals' intense pain and slaughter.

A graffiti-covered, vandalised swing,
A broken-down seesaw and a grey rubber ring.
A long, squeaky, slippery slide,
With room underneath for children to hide.

There is also a perfectly manicured bowling green,
Watched over by the park keeper,
(The guy's really mean).

Nearby, geese and swans swim on the pond,
Rabbits play in their hutch,
(Animals of which we are fond).

An aviary full of birds from here and far away,
Next to a playground where young
(and old!) children play.

People walk happily near the flowers and green trees,
The head gardener smiles. ('We aim to please!')

Nicola Foster (13)
Hurworth School

THE LOST LOVE

You left me with heartache
Lying by myself staring up
At a bare ceiling.

In the pitch black
I still see your face, looking,
Smiling with your tender lips.

I walk in from a walk
And see my place has been
Taken by another.

You looked at my face
And saw the hurt
All you can do is laugh.

When I came home to
Face the music,
Your things were gone,
You left me.

Sarah-Jane Brown (13)
Hurworth School

MY MUM

My mum is very nice
She smiles all the time.
Her cheeks are always red
But she always looks fine.

When she comes in from work
She flops down in a chair.
Sometimes she gets cross
When we tease her about her hair.

Every night she cooks our tea
And cleans the house right through.
She's always willing to help with homework
And feeding the animals too.

I love her very much
She's always good fun.
To me she's the one and only
World's best mum!

Laura Bernstone (13)
Hurworth School

NIGHT

As the sun sets, in the evening's grey light,
Pulling with it the deepest dark veil of night.
As the moon starts its shining,
And the stars start to sing,
The dark sweeps the land like a bird on the wing.

The land is all silent all lost in its sleep,
Not a creature is stirring, not even a peep.
The night pulls its darkness all over the land,
The azure sea lies slapping the sand.

The towering oak trees stand silent and lost,
Probed by the sparkling white fingers of frost.
As the grass waves a welcome,
To the incoming dew,
The sun rises up again golden and new.

Alice Smith (13)
Hurworth School

FLIGHT OF THE GIANT

Laying like a leviathan,
Spanning great distance over the solid ground.

Under the cover of an enormous dwelling place,
The ingress of cold steel,
Cantering to an open position.

A vehicle of incomparable size,
Ushered into the open air by a small controlled tug,
Led to another place of temporary rest.

A giant of considerable power,
Able to conquer large expanses of distance.

Despite this it takes but two people to control the beast,
From inside of its swelled frontage.

Then with a screech and a roar,
The creature burst into action,
Speeding along the surface.

With a bound it rose into the air,
Up and up through thermals and clouds,
Levelling at an unimaginable height.

By this time a place is in sight for it to land and
for people to alight,
At the end of he day it's done its job,
A plane that carries the holiday mob.

Daniel McDowell (13)
Hurworth School

THE GRAND CANYON

The sun slowly dying,
The heat is still frying.

The red sky like blood,
Where the great canyon stood.

The steady drop in light,
But the cliffs are still bright.

The water ripples,
The light trickles . . . away.

The cliffs no longer red,
Because the sun's dead.

Darkness . . . now just darkness.

What was once sunny and bright,
Has now turned to night.

Darkness is here,
But do not fear.

The light will be back . . . the light will be back.

The reds and the yellows,
Mix like orange Jell-O.

As the sun returns,
It brightly burns.

The sun seemed to fly
Across the blood-red sky.

But soon the sun will again die,
And we will say goodbye . . . say goodbye.

Philip Masters (13)
Hurworth School

SCHOOL

School is like a prison,
Classrooms are hot and stuffy as the sun,
Or cold like a refrigerator,
With blackboards as old as the teachers.

Lunchtimes are visiting times,
When people talk to their friends.
No parents. Just friends and enemies.
The noise is deafening, like the Commons.

The food is disgusting,
Mashed potato is green like gooey slime,
The bacon has lots of fat like worms
wriggling in and out.
The carrots are as hard as a rock.

The teachers are like rattlesnakes,
Never wanting to be disturbed,
And if they are, you can be sure
You will have a detention as long as a century.

Lessons are the worst.
These are tortures as bad as a prison sentence.
You are in a prison cell,
And you feel like a prune sitting alone working.

We have five a day.
That's *five* whole hours of pure death a day.
When all the teachers sit and glare at you,
And burn a hole in your head!

The end of the day is the best,
The bell goes and you can't wait to get out,
You pack your bag and rush for the door,
But then the teacher shouts . . .

'Hold it! Hold it! Halt!
Nobody leaves this cell until everything's put away.'
'Put the bars back on the windows,
Leave the skull in the corner,
I'll clean it up tomorrow!'

Emma Todd (13)
Hurworth School

LAKES

The waters lay still
in the basins they fill,
bottomless caves
under tumbling waves.

People in boats
steering clear, they float,
round the edge of the lake
like icing on a cake.

The clear blue sheet
rippled by feet,
hands dangle down
but make not a sound.

Gradually they leave
their boats they do heave,
out of the lake
themselves they take.

Now it is still
its place by the hill,
that towers above
like a fox over a dove.

Rosalyn Smith (13)
Hurworth School

DAYBREAK

Walking through the fallen leaves,
That cover the woodland path.
Winding through the naked trees,
With their towering outstretched branches.
The sun has not yet risen,
The chill wind numbs my face,
A startled bird flaps away,
Disturbing the peace with its race.
A squirrel scampers up a tree,
A rabbit hops in play.
A flock of geese fly overhead,
Welcoming the day.
The first rays of light,
Peek through the trees,
Casting shadows on the ground.
From behind its cloudy quilt of night,
Emerges a bright blue sky.

Laura Chapman (14)
Hurworth School

HEDGEHOGS

Sharp and prickly,
Round and brown,
Rolling round and round the ground.

Scurrying through the crunchy leaves,
In the cold and windy breeze,
Sniffing for grubs,
To fill their tums.

Before they say *good night!*

Amy Sedgwick (11)
Hurworth School

SATAN'S KINGDOM

The floors are strewn with the rotting remains
Of sinners past and present.
An infestation of bloodthirsty creatures
Scavenge across the wreckage
Of an ongoing massacre of human souls,
Like insects to scraps of food.

The soul is incised and torn apart
And fed to Satan's pet.
A savage, growling beast just waiting to claim a victim.
It devours the soul, draining the hope
And casting out the faith,
So all that is left is evil
Upon our foolish race.

Dragged through a tunnel of twisted cries
It crashed upon his domain.
The light of the world is plunged into darkness
And we can worship it no more.
Satan rose from his mighty kingdom
And wrapped crushing arms around the world.
All that's left is an eternal pit of death
And the massacre is complete.

Chris Devlin (13)
Hurworth School

THAT CERTAIN GUY

To be in his boots is any man's dream,
When he wears them, the sign from God is a sunbeam.
Those blue little triangles and those white *Reebok* letters,
Me and most of my friends would die if he met us.

Nothing can stop him as he takes on all men,
Look at him go he's gone past 10.
He's made a break he's on the offence,
He tears straight through any defence.

He can shoot from long range as it hits the inside of the pole,
It deflects straight on . . . incredible goal.
He earns 20 grand a week and not a penny less
And if you don't know who I'm talking about ,
You'll just have to guess.

He owns a cafe, a mansion and a very high pay,
Just remember every Saturday is the Welsh Wizard's Day.
He's got curly black hair and a really cool car
And he used to play with Eric Cantona.

He may not go out with one of the Spice Girls,
But he's friendly and Welsh and his hair's full of curls.
He likes lamb and he doesn't like figs,
If you haven't guessed, it's Ryan Giggs.

Adam Wilkinson (13)
Hurworth School

WAITING!

Stood around waiting,
Waiting for some answers,
Another one comes in.
They rush to its side,
Like a pin to a magnet,
Doors flap behind them, everything's quiet again,
Like a stone thrown in a pond left to rest.
Come on, what are they doing?
I became immune to the sound of them,
The standing stopped and the pacing began.
Up and down, 'Coffee sir?'
Said a voice, which seemed to be in my head.
I looked through the door,
Through the steamed-up window,
Beeeeeeeeeep -
I took a step back, the buzzing in my head,
'I'm sorry sir.'
I went blank and walked out.

Pippa Baker (14)
Hurworth School

STORM ON THE ISLAND

The storm is growing bigger and bigger
The wind is thrashing harder and harder
The trees are swaying more and more
The leaves are falling to the floor
The fences are leaning to one side
The rain is pouring down
The storm attacking everything
And then it dies away.

Steven Jamieson (15)
Hurworth School

BLACKPOOL

The tall tower stands up,
So everyone passing can look,
And it's what they all come to see.
In a world of its own,
It stands all alone,
But it's what they all come to see.

On go the lights,
Lighting the town at great heights,
For everyone around to see.
In their colours of red, orange, and yellow too
And their different shapes and sizes so new,
They light up the town for everyone to see.

Down the slide,
Like a rollercoaster ride,
As bumpy as can be
You look like a fool,
As you enter the pool,
But you're as happy as can be.

Blackpool's the place for me.

Gemma Lonsdale (13)
Hurworth School

ON A NIGHT

On a night when the sun has gone down and the sky has gone black,
I look up at the sky,
And in that sky, I see white dot stars,
But one day one star will be gone,
That star is Earth
With a bang, a boom, flash of light, it will all have gone!

David Ellis (14)
Hurworth School

POLLY AND ME

When you're walking through the countryside,
You may hear a scream,
That lovely peace was broken,
By a devastating scene.
It's really quite embarrassing,
But I simply just can't stop,
When Polly sets her mind to it,
I think someday she might pop.

She gallops faster, faster, faster,
Never stopping, just keeps on going,
As the world is whizzing by,
Polly speeds up with a hedge approaching.
We're not so good at stopping yet,
So here is the result,
Me flying through the air,
With a triple somersault.

Here's the place I know too well,
Me on the grass, all broken bones,
While Polly carries on.
'Not again!' The hospital moans.
After X-rays, off I go,
Back to riding my crazy friend,
We'll be together till the end.

Jane Brazier (14)
Hurworth School

The Storm

The sea was peaceful all day long
The clouds turned black and moody
The wind was a gentle breeze
It blew and blew to make the trees shake.

The sea scrambled up the beach to see
How far it could get. The sea was irritable.
It looked as if it could destroy the largest
of animals.

The trees swayed to and fro, savagely
Rain began to pour down
Getting heavier as it poured down.

The trees were twisted by the wind
The trees cling to the ground trying to
Survive through the storm.

The wind howled as it shook the windows
Suddenly with a gust of wind, a tree fell and its
Roots came with it. Crash! Bang! The tree
was down.

The wind howled with laughter as the
Tree tumbled to the ground. I was safe in
My house for now, or was I?

Samantha Cooper (14)
Hurworth School

THE STORM

It was Christmas Eve,
Snow was on the ground,
Thick grey clouds were above.
It started to become frosty,
So I went inside.

The wind picked up,
The tree branches were thumping on my window.
I nodded off,
I was surely tired.

The wind awoke me,
The snow had turned to water,
Rain and hail were falling rapidly.
The wind at this point,
Was knocking down bins.

The trees were still rattling against my window,
Help! Help! It was like I was surrounded.
The rain stopped,
The wind became still,
I fell back to sleep.
Now all was calm and quiet,
I could rest in peace.

Victoria Paver (14)
Hurworth School

LITTLE HEDGEHOG

Don't cross the road
Little hedgehog
You might get squashed
Little hedgehog
Stay on the pavement
Little hedgehog
Where you'll be safe
Little hedgehog
Oh no
Little hedgehog
You went on the road
Little hedgehog
And now you might be squashed
Little hedgehog
Oh phew
Little hedgehog
You didn't get squashed
Little hedgehog
I'm so glad
Little hedgehog
Now go back to your den
Little hedgehog
Where you'll be safe
Little hedgehog.

Kayleigh Evans (11)
Hurworth School

TRAPPED

Trapped,
Like how your body feels,
When it's addicted to a drug,
You can't lose it or shake it off.

Trapped,
In a world of fighting and killing,
You can't escape,
You can't break free.

Trapped,
In a place where no one will listen,
No one will help,
When all you want to do is talk.

Trapped,
Like an animal in a zoo,
When all that animal wants to do
Is walk around.

Trapped,
Your feelings,
When they're bottled up inside,
Wanting to express themselves.

Trapped,
In a hospital when you're ill,
When all you want,
Is to be well.

All of these things have one thing in common,
They all yearn for freedom.

Lucy Todd (12)
Hurworth School

THE STORM

It was a cold morning,
frost lay on the ground.
No clouds in the sky,
It was so quiet.

Then the clouds arrived,
it went all dark.
The wind blew, rain came down,
the trees started to sway.

Trees across the road swayed,
rain bounced off the road.
Then crash, a tree fell,
blocking up the road.

The beck was rising,
no one could get out.
The bridge began to disintegrate,
the river had broken its bank.

People rushing everywhere,
trying to get furniture to high places.
Making sand bags,
getting everything to high places.

All the pots to be stacked,
coffee tables to go up,
My dad's model planes,
the pets to go upstairs.

Nightfall came,
everyone was up.
The following morning,
it was so quiet, not a soul was in sight.

We didn't go to school that day,
no one could get across the bridge.
The house was a mess,
everything went quiet,
the storm had gone.

Jennifer Sanderson (14)
Hurworth School

WONDERING

I sit alone,
The dark night past,
Wondering,
What a new day would be like.
Sleepless nights,
Cold and wet rain, tip, tat, tip, tat,
I stay awake,
Wondering, wondering.
The dogs howling,
Cold and unhappy,
Laying awake,
Wind howling,
Wondering.
What would the future hold,
Another day past.
Watching the night go by,
Another night,
I sit alone.
Wondering, wondering.

Emma Paver (11)
Hurworth School

NO ONE LIKES RATS!

Leopards are spotty,
Whales are blue,
Kittens are cute,
And puppies are too.

Parrots are squawky,
Hyenas are chatty,
Pigs are talky,
And lemmings are just batty.

Bears are furry,
Chipmunks are fast,
Cats are purry,
But no one likes rats.

Heather Minto (11)
Hurworth School

HEDGEHOG

Hedgehog
Sleeps anywhere
In a bush
In a ditch
It does not
Matter which
By a river
Where he shivers
Hedgehogs
Sleep anywhere
Anywhere,
Shhh shhh.

Kelly Pybus (12)
Hurworth School

PIGS

Pigs are fat,
Pigs are round,
Pigs make an oinking sound.
Pigs are pink,
Pigs are brown,
Pigs are clean,
Do not frown.
Pigs are great,
Pigs are sweet,
Pigs have trotters,
For their feet.
Pigs are fat,
Pigs are good,
Pigs like rolling,
In the mud!

Gemma Roberts (11)
Hurworth School

SCHOOL

It's that day again 'Monday'!
That awful day again.
The fearsome smell
As if it was hell.
Sitting lonely
Children screaming, messing about
While I sit working, thinking.
Hard to concentrate with the storm
Smashing outside the window.
It's that day again 'Monday'!
That awful day again.

David Gowling (13)
Hurworth School

LADYBIRDS

Hiding among the grass,
I wait for them to pass,
Then suddenly,
They've found me,
Hiding among the grass.

They begin to crawl,
'Oh no!' Here's my brother with his ball,
If I pounce,
He won't bounce,
But I'm hiding among the grass.

Over my buckle,
Then down, they scuttle,
I love to watch ladybirds,
While hiding among the grass.

Samantha Young (11)
Hurworth School

BIRDS EAT

Birds eat
Anywhere
On rooftops
At the fair
On the ground
They don't care.
Birds eat
Anywhere.
Birds fly in the sky
Or they're made into a pie.

Paul Brentley (11)
Hurworth School

THE UNLUCKY FARMER

Once I saw some pigs
Eating cheese and figs
Afterwards for sweet
They had a strawberry treat
Another day
They ran away
And left their homes behind
The farmer said
They must be dead
No more ham today.

Once I saw some sheep
They jumped a big wool heap
Another day
They ran away
And left their homes behind
The farmer said
They must be dead
No more lamb today.

Katie Hayllar (11)
Hurworth School

RELAXING

I sunk into my pillows,
switched on the TV.
Grabbed my cup of cocoa,
and that just settled me!

Laura Ward (11)
Hurworth School

WITHOUT YOU

Silence is my sound without you.
My life is worth nothing without you.
The world means nothing without you.
Tears on my face without you.

My life is worth nothing.
But my heart won't stop beating.
Why don't you love me as I love you?

You mean everything to me,
But I mean nothing to you.
I'll always love you,
I only wish you'd love me too.

Silence is my sound without you,
Tears on my face without you,
Dark is my day without you.

I can't eat without thinking about you,
I can't think without you,
I can't sleep without thinking about you.

Love will mean nothing to me until I get you.

Toni Leach (11)
Hurworth School

WHY

Why are people killing me?
Why don't they care?
Don't they realise what they're doing?
Soon we'll all be rare.
From cars spew out exhaust fumes,
Indoors there's smoking in rooms.

Taking in drugs at the age of seven,
Less and less people go up to heaven.
Around the town, a dangerous smell
More and more people go down to hell.
Once it's done, it's total disaster,
We can't mend it with a magic plaster.

Ben Chapel (13)
Hurworth School

CARS!

Cars are great,
They never make you late,
Unless they break,
Or get driven into a lake.

There's Ferrari's, Skoda's, Lada's and Ford's,
But there's one car that will make you bored,
It's a Toyota Corolla,
You'd be very ashamed even if you won it in a tombola.

Even Jeremy Clarkson said
'It's more exciting to stay in bed.'
But there's one worse car you can get,
It's an old and rusty Vauxhall Chevette,
But when it breaks down,
All you can do is frown.

Performance cars are great,
The speed and ability is given to you on a plate,
Cars, cars, they're great to drive,
When they're tuned, it's like they come alive.

Peter Hedley (11)
Hurworth School

QUICK! STOP!

Quick! There's a flood,
Build a dam!
Stop! Forget the dam,
There's a drought!

Quick! Find some water,
There's a fire!
Stop! There's no water,
The drought!

Quick! Build a well,
We need water!
Stop! We can't dig,
Get some tools!

Quick! Get help,
Burst pipe!
Stop! Forget the help,
Bring a cloth!

Quick! Get help now,
This isn't working!
Stop! One more try.
Bring another cloth!

Quick! Help me,
I'm soaking!
Stop! Find some help,
Go and get someone!

Quick, Get a move on,
I'm dying here!
Stop! I give up,
Let's move!

Laura Todd (11)
Hurworth School

HAMSTER

Hamsters nibble anything,
Anything they find,
A couch,
A chair,
Maybe a teddy bear.

They swing,
They hang,
And make a bang.

They don't care,
They play,
        anywhere.

Vicki Richards (11)
Hurworth School

SPIDER

A spider
Called Fred
Is dead.
He lived
On my wall
Proud and tall.
He died.

When alive
He loved to dive
From my light
To give me
A fright
In the dead
Of night.

Richard Carlin (11)
Hurworth School

Football, Football It's All I Dream

If I could be a football player,
Then a football player I'd be.
It's all I dream and think about,
At dinner and at tea.

If I could play for Leeds United
And maybe England too,
All my dreams would be answered,
And maybe all my nightmares too?

I have to do maths and English,
And so I toss and turn in bed.
My thoughts keep going back to
I'd rather play football instead!

Michael Chapman (11)
Hurworth School

Dogs

Dogs drool anywhere
Any table, any chair
They don't care
Anywhere
Dogs drink anything
From tea to
Coffee, they don't
Care so, I thought
You ought to know
So don't leave
Your drink all
Over the show.

Daniel Cooper (11)
Hurworth School

WHISP

My dog Whisp has big brown eyes
A dark, damp nose that often pries.
Into places that are forbidden
And very often, very well hidden.
A patch of mud is all that shows
Of places that she shouldn't go.

A bark that terrifies
A bite that destroys
As another paper becomes one of her toys.
She may be small
But she's never slow
Mention the world *'walk'* and off she'll go.

One ear up and one ear down
A waggy tail that won't quite touch the ground.
A welcoming bark you'll always get
From my very favourite pet.

Jennie Haines (11)
Hurworth School

I HATE FROGS

I hate frogs I really do!
I'd scream if I found one in the loo.
They're orange, blue, green and red.
I'd die if I found one in my bed.
I legged it when I saw a toad.
And then it got squashed on the road.
I hate frogs, I really do!
They're green and slimy,
And smell like you . . . !

Holly Avery (11)
Hurworth School

FREEDOM

Freedom is a lion,
Not locked up in a zoo,
But roaming the plains of Africa,
As lions are meant to do.

Freedom is an eagle,
Not tethered to a man,
But soaring from the mountains,
Part of God's eternal plan.

Freedom is a monkey,
Not in a wire cage,
But swinging from the treetops,
No matter what his age.

Freedom is the countryside,
In various hues of green,
Never to be developed,
But always to be seen.

Freedom is the human race,
A mix of black, brown and white,
With each and every one of us,
Having equal rights.

Stephanie Hiley (12)
Hurworth School

JET

I've got a dog who runs like a gale
He's got a propeller, also known as his tail
Every time he spins it round
He zooms off at the speed of sound

When he's tired and can't run anymore
He goes in the kitchen for dog-food galore
Then when old Jet has had his fill
He knocks the cat off the window-sill.

John Ilee (11)
Hurworth School

SNAKES

Snakes slither
anywhere
under the table
under the chair
top of a cage
in your shoe
anybody's bin will do.
Beneath the drawers
under the bed
just be careful
where you tread.
Over the pillows
between the sheets
watch out or it will
nip your feet.
Down the stairs
into the hall
anywhere
they don't care
snakes slither
anywhere.

Victoria McKone (11)
Hurworth School

The English Room's Death

Mrs Johnson is a teacher who is very proud.
Because you see her class are loud-mouthed,
We've read and read,
Until we nearly dropped dead,
Now we will write and write,
Until our knuckles turn white,
So if you see us going out of the room,
Please don't come in, it will be your doom,
So a warning to everyone, keep out, keep out,
If you don't listen, we will shout,
Keep out! Keep out!
Please don't go, don't even stray,
Keep out of the room, it will be your doom.

Rachael Evans (11)
Hurworth School

Freedom

Freedom is doing what you want,
Living your life to the full,
Every day is a new day,
Doing what you like to do,
Forget all the past, when you were alone,
Freedom is good, you're not always at home,
Everyone is free,
Everyone has freedom,
I am free,
I am me,
Freedom is doing what you want to do,
That's why I'm me.

Rachel Hastie (12)
Hurworth School

WHAT IS FREEDOM?

Freedom is . . .

Relaxing in front of the TV,
On a cold winter's night.
The space all around you,
The wind blowing in your hair.
Choosing what you want from life,
Getting your own way.
Getting in the bathroom before your sister,
And never having to wash your face.
Wearing what you want.
Holidays in the warm summer's sun.
It's your life,
Live it how you want.
        Have freedom!

Rachel Lambert (12)
Hurworth School

FREEDOM

Freedom is where you can have peace and quiet
Where you can do whatever you want to do
Lots of people have their freedom
And don't ever realise it until it's gone.
But this is not everyone's idea of freedom
Some people want to run and play
Some people want to be alone
Some people want to travel the world
Or not go to school.
You are free to choose what your freedom is.

Lisa McCready (12)
Hurworth School

AMERICA

When I went to America,
I got quite a scare,
When I found out,
How long it would take to get there!

The day that we got there,
We went out,
We went to the shops,
To have a look about.

When we got back,
We watched TV,
There were too many adverts,
So I yelled, *'Dear me!'*

The billboards,
They are huge and bright,
And they all,
Light up at night.

The burgers,
They are really big,
They must think,
I am a pig.

I had some pancakes,
For my tea,
They gave me not one,
But they gave me three!

But I don't care,
America's the one for me.

Steven Wilson (12)
Hurworth School

FREEDOM

You are free
To do what you want to do
Live your life
To do what you want to do.
I am free
Just me and no more you.
Break free
To do what you please.
Be free
No more begging on your knees.
Life is freedom
Lots of space.
Life is freedom
Freedom is ace.
Say what you want,
Freedom is free,
Just being me,
I love being free.

Lyndsey Shaw (12)
Hurworth School

DOGS

A dog is very friendly, it is also very bright,
It meets you on a morning,
It meets you on a night,
Its tail can tell you if it's happy,
It tells you when it's sad,
A dog is a friend forever,
A friend, I am glad to have.

Vickie Wetherill (12)
Hurworth School

PUPPIES

Puppies will go anywhere,
A lion's cave,
They don't care.
Through a river,
Through the sea,
To fetch some silly thing for me.
They'll even travel
Through the snow,
Anywhere,
That's where they'll go.
Through a forest,
Through the trees,
Even being,
Chased by bees.
I've said it once,
I'll say it again,
They'll wander through
A lion's den.
Yes puppies will go anywhere,
Anywhere!
'Cos they don't care.

Mike Brazier (11)
Hurworth School

FREEDOM

Out go my parents,
the TV is free,
I lean for the controller,
and turn on the TV.

On comes the football,
I'm having fun.
Newcastle score,
I drop my cream bun.

Oh no there is cream
all over the floor.
Then I hear footsteps,
coming through the door.

Freedom is gone,
my parents are back.
I turn off the TV,
and go and hit the sack.

Mark Swanwick (13)
Hurworth School

FREEDOM

Is freedom going on holiday?
Just wandering around with nobody.
Is freedom being able to fly?
Or living forever, never to die?
Is freedom being able to speak?
Or not having a wash and staring to reek!

   Is that freedom?

If none of these are freedom, not one of these things,
Is it like an eagle with gigantic wings,
Soaring through the sky doing loops and things?

   How can I tell?

I found out what is freedom,
It's what you desire,
Freedom is a feeling,
Freedom is a fire.

   That's what freedom is?

Daniel Haggart (12)
Hurworth School

FREEDOM!

Freedom!
Freedom is space,
Space is a never-ending nothing,
A nothing that hovers there.
Freedom,
Freedom of what to see,
Freedom of believing what you want to believe.
It's just freedom.

Freedom!
Freedom in life,
Life is a room that does not yet exist.
Freedom,
Freedom of whatever!
Freedom or whatever happens in life.
Freedom,
It's just freedom.

Freedom!
Freedom of your expressions.
Expressions of feelings,
Feelings of anger, sadness and happiness,
Freedom,
Freedom is crying,
Crying and never wanting to stop,
Freedom,
It's just freedom.

Patricia Machin (12)
Hurworth School

ANIMAL FREEDOM

Freedom is a horse,
galloping round and round.
Freedom is a kangaroo,
hopping on the ground.
Freedom is a lion,
lying in a crowd.
It's a pig lying in a bound.

Freedom isn't an animal locked-up.
Freedom isn't cruel.
Freedom is nice.
Freedom is full of joy and happiness.
Not sadness and loneliness.

Freedom is a monkey,
swinging from trees.
Freedom is a cat,
having a mad half-hour.
Freedom is a mouse,
getting covered in flour.
Freedom is a tiger,
using his power.

Freedom is space,
all around animals.
Room for them,
to run, hide and play.
Room for animals,
to have a great day.
Not boring and scary
But a place for them to stay!

Claire Fletcher (13)
Hurworth School

FREEDOM

Freedom for a polar bear,
Is to roam free,
Walk anywhere,
And everywhere,
No bars to stop him.

But he's trapped,
Kept in,
Five paces up,
Five paces down,
No more, no less.

He gets a new enclosure,
Keeper says it's good,
But it is still,
Five paces up,
Five paces down,
No more, no less.

He's never known freedom,
Been trapped all his life,
Five paces up,
Five paces down,
No more, no less.

Jane Sutcliffe (13)
Hurworth School

WHEN MY PONY'S ILL

When my pony is ill
My mum rings the vet
He comes the same day and says
'Oh what a pet.'

'What seems to be the matter
with this poor old pony?'
We tell him, he explains
she'll be fine in a moment.
He gives her an injection
and says 'Perfection.'
She'll be as right as rain.

Suzanne Carter (13)
Hurworth School

FREEDOM

What is freedom?
Such a strange word,
Sounds quite absurd!
Riding in the sun,
Having such fun,
What is freedom?
Such a strange word,
Sounds quite absurd!
Seeing the moon rise,
Watching as the owl flies,
What is freedom?
Such a tempting word,
Sounds almost absurd!
Lying on the cool grass,
With a beautiful lass,
What is freedom?
Such a strange magic word,
Sounds totally absurd!

Kevin Smith (12)
Hurworth School

FREEDOM

I see the eagle swooping low,
The eagle's free,
Not like me,
Polar bears roaming the icy slopes,
Laughing hyenas,
Making jokes,
Oh! How I'd love to be,
The king of all the sea,
Free to go where I want, nothing can come near me.
I look at the lion in a cage, it's so unfair,
He should be running,
With the wind in his hair,
No worries in the world,
A penguin in Antarctica,
Playing in the snow,
A wild cat,
Stalking through the trees,
That cat's free,
Not like me.

Catherine Bennison (12)
Hurworth School

FREEDOM

F lying like an eagle in a deep blue sky.
R earing like a horse trying to fly.
E very newborn baby.
E very blooming flower.
D oing what you want to do.
O r running through a grass meadow.
M aking believe, I'm free.

Ben Robertson (12)
Hurworth School

THAT'S WHAT SISTERS ARE FOR!

Even though you cause me stress,
It doesn't mean I love you any less,
Sometimes you don't sleep at night,
But I'll sit with you till morning light.

You're my only sister,
And I love you a lot,
Even though we fight like cat and dog,
I still love you.

I know you can't help what you're doing,
But your medicine will help you,
You have epilepsy,
And you mean a lot,
I just can't bear to lose what I've got.

Louise Roxby (13)
Hurworth School

NOWHERE TO GO

I'm trapped in a cage all alone,
No one to speak to,
And nowhere to go,
There are footsteps on the grass,
But no one to speak to, and nowhere to go.
There is a rustling in the trees,
But no one to speak to,
And nowhere to go.
A man lets me out,
Someone to speak to
And a home to go to.

Liam Robertson (12)
Hurworth School

FREEDOM

Freedom is floating
Swiftly in the air.
Freedom is scribbling
On your work without a care.
Freedom is eating
Scrumptious cream cakes.
Freedom is taking
A stroll down by the lakes.

Freedom is having
Loads of money.
Freedom is every day
Being hot and sunny.
Freedom is cooling down
In a swimming pool.
Freedom is never to
Have to go to school.

Christina Fossheim (12)
Hurworth School

FREEDOM

Free as a bird, going where you want.
Free to do whatever you want to do.
Free is having loads of cash,
and going on a spending spree.
Free is thinking what you like, and not in danger.
Free is running in wide open spaces,
with no obstructions in your way.
Free is jumping anywhere!
Free is not being locked away,
in a dark, dark cellar

David Ralph (12)
Hurworth School

FOOTBALL

The crowd screaming
like a chalk on a blackboard,
The stadium shaking
like an old man with schizophrenia,
The smell of the pie and peas
rings around the seats that we sit in.

The game's going well,
we're 2-0 up.
Just 3 minutes to go,
the final whistle blows.
We've won the game.
Winners roar with excitement,
losers boo in shame.

Tim Covell (13)
Hurworth School

FREEDOM

Freedom is being able to do,
Whatever you want,
It's staying up late,
Lying in, in the morning,
No school,
All holidays,
Freedom is kind,
Freedom is peaceful,
Freedom is free.

Rachael Pitt (12)
Hurworth School

SPIDERS

Spiders ugh, spiders, big, small or hairy,
Why do they always seem so scary?
They crawl across your ceilings,
Run along your floor,
And when that one's run off, there's more.
Spiders ugh, spiders, with webs that catch their prey.
Silky string-like cotton,
How does it get that way?
They slide along your bath tubs,
Run along your stairs.
Then when you start screaming,
They are gone.
They're not there.

Heidi Fleary (13)
Hurworth School

FREEDOM

F is for the fun we shared when we were little,
R is for the times we ran through the meadows,
E is for the endless laughs we had together,
E is for the enemies we had forever,
D is when we didn't have any homework,
O is for the only world we knew,
M is for the memories I had to keep,
　　when our freedom was taken away.

Emma Lowrie (13)
Hurworth School

FREEDOM

My parents are out
I am all on my own.
But the TV's not working
I wish they'd come home.
I'm starving with hunger,
and I can't cook a bone.

It's been an hour now
no telephone call.
Something has happened
a stray cannon ball?
I try to think about nice things
it doesn't work at all.

Ring, ring goes the phone
jump out of my skin.
I've spilled all my Coke
right into the bin.
I pick up the phone 'Is anyone in?'
'Yes it's me David,'
'I just wondered who is in.'

In the door comes my mother
after her, follows my brother.
'Mum can I have some tea'
my brother shouts, 'And for me.'

David it's time for bed
I go upstairs and put down my head.

Mark Flood (13)
Hurworth School

Love And Peace

Spirit of love, spirit of light,
Wave your magic spell tonight.
Heal the rift, stop the fight,
Help us see, in love's delight.

> *Love and peace.*

Let there be love, let there be light,
Wave your wand all through the night,
Help the people stop and fight.
Let them see through the night

> *Love and peace.*

It's all about love and peace,
Let him lie in perfect peace.
Help him see, keep him away from
that nasty beast.

> *Love and peace.*

Let him live and don't let him die,
If you do, I will fall and cry.
Help in fight in shepherds' delight,
Make sure he is alright.

> *Love and peace.*

Krystle Shields (14)
Hurworth School

Autumn

Coloured leaves falling from the trees,
With the help from an autumn breeze,
With frost on the pavement and dew on the grass,
Me and my friends having a laugh.

Darker mornings, darker nights,
Hallowe'en is a fright,
Witches and ghosts shouting *'Trick or treat'*
I am snuggled up in the lovely heat.

Jenna Taylor (13)
Hurworth School

WAR

In the middle of the night,
I start from a dream.
The only one left,
To hear my scream.

Out of the shelter,
Into the din.
Bombs, shrapnel, bullets,
Closing me in.

The town echoes,
The English fight.
But the Germans still battle,
And screams fill the night.

I feel so helpless,
I huddle and I moan.
But when all is over,
I might still be here, alone.

A strange smell wanders,
Through the dark night.
But still the bombs keep coming,
And I wish I could fight!

Craig Buckley (13)
Hurworth School

FIRE

Fire burning everywhere,
Up the curtains,
On the chair,
Sparks are sizzling in my hair.

It was my home,
It was my place,
Now it's in a dreadful state.

The fire brigade arrived too late,
Saw the mess,
Tried their best,
Even sorted all the rest.

Now I've no home,
But soon, some day,
I'll write a new poem
When I've found a new way.

Nichola Harkness (13)
Hurworth School

BACK TO SCHOOL

I hate it when we go back to school.
We don't even have a swimming pool.
More pencils, more books,
More teachers giving ugly looks.
There's a new teacher in,
I wonder if she'll be teaching me?
When you're feeling down,
The teachers will bring you round.
The cane has been reinstated,
I wonder whose hand prints will be on it first?

John Sunter (13)
Hurworth School

I Wish You Were Mine

She could dance
She could fly
She could score a try

She could throw
She could catch
She could throw a big bash

Oh I wish you were mine

We've known each other
What seems to be like forever
But it's still not long enough

Please, please be mine for all time.

Lee Marsh (14)
Hurworth School

Chocolate

C is for all the chocolate in the world.
H is for the happiness of getting one.
O is for the original taste.
C is for crying out for more.
O is for oozing in chocolate spread.
L is for lapping up chocolate drinks.
A is for the appetising taste.
T is for the tantalising of your tastebuds afterwards.
E is for the everlasting supply.

Chocolate is the best thing in the world.

Helen Easby (14)
Hurworth School

Freedom

I like to see horses galloping free,
Don't want to be barred up under lock and key,
Grazing silently in the sun,
Bucking and rearing having such fun.
Their strong bodies with sleek soft fur,
Ribs not scarred by whip or spur.
Then a man comes to take them away
From where they used to gallop and play.
Now his worst nightmare has come
How could he have been so dumb?
To be caught by a man and lead away
To somewhere he'll be forced to stay.

Kathryn Williams (12)
Hurworth School

The Storm

The wind howls like lost souls screaming,
Am I awake or am I dreaming?
I hear the sound of the raging sea,
Like a distant echo calling to me.
It has no pity, it has no remorse,
Mother Nature must take her course.
In wild abandon, it devours all
And to its power the mighty fall.
The ravaged rocks surrender to the tide,
Like an eager virgin bride.
Who knows what terror lies
Beneath the dark unforgiving skies.

Manuela Hairsine (14)
Hurworth School

THUNDER

Thump, thump, thump
Striding towards us a *T-Rex*
It towered thirty feet
Above the trees
Each thigh a ton of meat.

He picked us up!
Examining us like toys
Hisssssss teeeeeeeth like daggers
He had left prints 6 inches deep.

'Fire' The man shouted
Bang! Bang! Bang!
The *T-Rex* fell with a big

Thud

And the jungle was silent.

Rachael Herdman (12)
Moorside Comprehensive School

THE STORM

In the darkness of the night,
The gods' light begins to flash,
The clouds begin to rumble,
As the light slashes and tumbles,
The light crashes into a tree,
The smoke and steam begin to rise into the misty skies,
Daft as a brush the tree topples over,
The lightning strikes as fast as light,
The fingers of the light touch a tree as cold as ice they may be.

Greg Roe (11)
Moorside Comprehensive School

MY LAST DAY

My life is hard, my life is sad
Why does it have to be so bad?
I trudge along a dusty road,
With my heavy, unbearable load.
My back is rubbed raw,
Where my bones stick out.
I've got to keep going though, I have no doubt.
This is a hot and miserable land,
Without the help of a kindly hand.
I really need a long cool drink,
I'll stop at this trough and have one, I think.
Hard hands stop me and pull me away,
I can't even have a drink today.
Everyone seems to be so rough,
I'm so tired and weak, I've had enough.
The road is stony, I'm getting lame,
I've had enough of work and pain.
I've laid down now on the dust and dirt,
A peace is coming, no more will I hurt.

Stacy Green (13)
Moorside Comprehensive School

TYRANNOSAURUS REX

The T-Rex strode through the woods,
Raising his mighty head,
His eyes rolling, left and right,
Searching for his food.

Trees crashing to the ground,
Every foot makes a hard pound,
It towered over all the trees,
Men weren't even up to its knees.

Its oily reptilian skin,
And its frail watchmaker's arms,
Its legs, each a piston,
Of a ton of white bone.

He let out a mighty roar,
Ready to rip asunder,
Each tooth, a very sharp dagger,
His roar was like deep thunder.

Steven Eccles (12)
Moorside Comprehensive School

THE SUBSTITUTE

My dad came in from work, got changed
and then carried me across the road
to the football field.

It was so big, I never went to the far end.
We stayed at the bottom and played in the goal,
a mile long and two storeys high.

We'd kick the ball between the two bright, white posts
as thick as tree trunks, I'd run and run until my dad said,
'Howay, ye tea'll be ready.'

I loved to watch him play on Sundays, for different teams
I wanted to grow up and play football
just like my dad.

I grew up playing for schools and teams.
Now it's he who comes to watch me.

Simon Scarr (15)
Moorside Comprehensive School

THE STORM

A storm crashed through a town,
It began to blow some trees down,
The wind howled through the rain,
Frightening people out of their skins again.

The houses shook from side to side,
All the children cried and cried,
Then all of a sudden the storm stopped,
And the force of the wind dropped.

The storm was now over,
All thanks to the person who wished on the
                                            four-leaf clover,
But now the town is as cold as ice,
Soon it should look as nice as nine pence.

Kirsty Grant (11)
Moorside Comprehensive School

THE STORM

The storm is a cruel monster
Rushing through the sky.

The storm is hard as iron
When it hits you on the thigh.

The storm is as cold as ice
When it blows off your hat.

The storm is really vicious
When it whistles through your flat.

Mandy Davison (11)
Moorside Comprehensive School

Death

A knock at the door
and saddened voices informed us
Granny was dead.
6 o'clock, in hospital was the time it happened.

I was just ten
when it came to the house.
It blew through
like a cold north wind.

I was young
I didn't understand.
All around people were sad
but I was not.

Mother said it was expected.
Arrangements were made,
Relatives came and went.

In the corner I sat,
trying to feel sad.
But the pain was soon gone.

Life must go on.

The funeral arrived and departed
but deep inside,

A saddened child still lives.

Craig Suddick (15)
Moorside Comprehensive School

An Animal's Way

The giraffe stands so tall and so very proud
The lion roars and likes to live in a crowd.
The sea-lion slides and swims all day
While the kangaroo just hops, skips and jumps away.

The elephant is large and never forgets
The bear is fierce and has no regrets.
The tiger is vain and full of pride
While the whale likes to swim on the deep and high tide.

The panda is soft and furry and large
The leopard crouches down ready to charge.
The koala is cuddly and climbs up high
While the moose has a mournful, sorrowful cry.

The hippo is big and gets his own way
The jaguar is fast and runs all day.
The ant-eater is shy and not well known
While most creatures are frightening when they are
                                            fully grown.

Kim Kirsopp (13)
Moorside Comprehensive School

As The Children Try To Fly

When I was eight,
I had a friend with a pirate smile,
Make-believe and play pretend,
We were innocent and wild.

Hopped my fence and slammed the gate,
Running down an alleyway,
As the children tried to fly.

On the dresser sits a frame,
With a photograph,
Two little girls in pony-tails,
Some long 6 years back.

I never saw that girl again,
She never ran back down that alleyway,
And *'still'* the children try to fly.

Lindsey Gibson (13)
Moorside Comprehensive School

T-REX

His large feet have killer claws,
One of them slices you and out your blood pours.
Each leg is made of large bone sunk in huge, tough muscle,
Every time he twitches a muscle, 10 trees' leaves will rustle.

At the back of his legs, an enormous fat tail,
One swing of it, could kill a whale.
Even animals with the loudest roars,
Cannot survive his watchmaker's claws.

All of his claws stab and tear,
One lash could kill the largest bear.
His snake-neck coiled, covered in slimy skin,
Which is as tough as metal or tin.

His head is a ton of bone,
As large as a tree, as hard as stone.
His powerful jaw and teeth, like daggers
could crush you like a berry.
So anything in his path is no longer merry.

Stephanie Graham (12)
Moorside Comprehensive School

My First Race

Tacking up my trotter.
The tension brewing.
Excitement in the air,
Up I get, feet in the stirrups,
hands on the reins.
My silks are shining in the sun.
My mam and dad, giving me a loving hug,
Then off I go trotting in my place.
My hands are shaking and my teeth
are chattering.
But old Falsehood has done this a thousand times.
So he is as calm as can be.
The start car, starts to pull away,
3,2,1 and they're off and pacing.

Rebecca Lister (13)
Moorside Comprehensive School

The T-Rex

The T-Rex came on striding legs,
Its eyes were as big as ostrich eggs.
Its legs were huge and it towered over the trees,
The hunters were as frightened as the swarming bees.

It came into the clearing, screaming and roaring,
Its voice was like aeroplanes, soaring.
It growled and its teeth crashed,
The sound was like glass had smashed.

Its scales were green and glistening,
The flies swarmed and the hunters stood listening.
Its skin was covered in slime,
The hunters shot it at the right time.

Gina Brewis (13)
Moorside Comprehensive School

FROM KENT TO KENT

When I went flying
I felt really excited
because it's nice to be invited.
I flap my wings
and give a puff
but the wind is far too rough.
I twist and turn
as the hurricane comes.
But I'm a bird
I'm very strong.
I'll get through it won't be long.
But the wind never settled and the wind never went
and I ended up, back in Kent!

Jemma Green (11)
Moorside Comprehensive School

TYRANNOSAURUS REX

It came on striding legs
And then towered thirty feet
A great evil god
With great fearsome teeth.

Each lower leg was a piston
Just like each eye, did glisten
A thousand pounds of white bone
Made all around tremble and moan.

We heard the great bang of a gun
And the monster it fell like a stone
Then Travis, his eyes, they shone
The monster before him was gone.

Victoria Clews (12)
Moorside Comprehensive School

I Want You

I want you always every minute I draw breath, I think of you,
your soft touch, your warm heart,
I want you always for as long as time goes on,
I want you through the daylight hours when you hold me close
to you.
I want you when you're sleeping and all through the night,
I want your good, I want your bad,
I want your pain, I want your love,
I want your every tiny detail no matter how small,
I want you, I need you, I love you, for our lives together are lived
as one.

Katie Brewis (13)
Moorside Comprehensive School

T-Rex

Ten tons of muscle
Pebbled skin
Teeth like daggers
A deathly grin
Empty eyes and taloned feet
Leaving footprints, six inches deep
An evil god
A deadly foe
A great tail, swinging to and fro
Crashing trees and rumbling ground
The thunder-lizard, looks around
Its snake-like neck
Its gliding step
There's no mistaking
The monstrous T-Rex.

Craig Rogerson (12)
Moorside Comprehensive School

BEATINGS

I was six when mum got knocked around.
He punched, he pulled, he pushed her
to the ground.

She scampered through the kitchen
and reached out for the phone.
By swinging his tattooed arm
he broke my mum's jawbone.

He threw her in the other room and
beat her up some more.
I leaned further over to get a view
and stumbled through the door.

He saw me scramble behind the couch
he shouted, 'Get to bed!'
Meanwhile, mum escaped his arms
and hit him on the head.

He stumbled a little towards me
while cursing at my mum.
I ran at him and pushed him away
he fell like a tree cut into chunks.

My brother, my mother and I
left him on the floor in a heap.
I hoped he'd die for the stunts that he pulled
I dreamt it in my sleep.

We have a new life now
he no longer causes us hurt.
His new wife will not take his blows
and is not treated like dirt.

Calvin Todd (15)
Moorside Comprehensive School

DEPRESSION

Lying on my bed
wondering what to do
thinking of things to cheer me up
but I can't think. Can you?

There's nothing to do here
nothing at all
my walls are collapsing
they're going to fall.

I feel like I'm dying
but I know that I'm not
it's called depression
this thing that I've got.

I've tried so hard
to make it go away
the only thing is
that *'it'* wants to stay!

It's ruining my life
but it won't anymore
I'm determined to go out
as I once did before.

I'll try to forget
the things that he said
then hopefully it will go
right out of my head.

Why did I listen
to someone like that?
He's out to ruin lives
but not mine, that's a fact.

My life was perfect
before he came along
and if I get my way
it'll be his that goes wrong!

Helen Alderson (15)
Moorside Comprehensive School

THE STORM

Lying in bed fast asleep suddenly there was an enormous crash
of thunder,
my ears ringing while it stops for a second *Bang!*
There it goes again, this was louder than the one before.

I got out of bed and walked to my window,
I saw the most awful thing, there were leaves and branches flying
around,
trees bending over, it looked like they were going to snap.

The wind was howling like a pack of wolves.
The lightning was touching the ground.

The car alarms were bleeping and babies were weeping
with the echoing thunder outside.
I ran out of my room to find my mum.
As I went along the corridor, my hair was blowing onto my face.
I turned and looked, shocked, the wind had blown the window out.

There was a sea of glass on the floor.
I stood frozen, like a block of ice waiting for someone to come.
I waited and waited and then the storm died down until it
eventually stopped.

Kerry Mordue (11)
Moorside Comprehensive School

She's Gone

Mother broke the bad news.
At first there was nothing.
I sat there in silence thinking about the situation.
While the others cried and hugged.
It seemed like forever.
But then all of a sudden.
A rush of tears flooded my eyes.
She was gone.

I couldn't eat, I couldn't sleep.
At night I would cry and cry,
Like a baby without its mother.
But only I was without my best friend.
My saviour, my grandmother.

I was in a daze all day.
While memories of us played in my mind.
I used to play with her wrinkled skin.
Soft as silk.
Used to curl up together on the sofa.
While watching TV, while I told her.
Secrets no other knew.
With our fingers entwined and arms.
Embracing one another, I felt safe, so loved.

I couldn't imagine life without her.
But it was happening.
There would be no more watching TV.
No more heartfelt hugs.
No more grandma.

There was a large piece of me lost that day.
I felt empty.
I cried and sobbed so much.
I almost became hysterical.
I couldn't cry any longer.
My eyes were so sore and
There were no more tears left to be cried.
She was gone.

Emma Dawson (15)
Moorside Comprehensive School

THE STORM

The colour of sky was as black as night,
Sam watched from the porthole
shaking with fright.

The lightning flashed,
and lit up the sky,
as the thunder clapped,
and the waves lashed high.

The ship tossed about on the stormy sea,
Sam wished there was somewhere else he could be.

The storm finally stopped and the sea became calm,
He hoped that his shipmates had come to no harm.

As pleased as punch,
filled his heart full of joy,
when he heard a voice shout *'Land ahoy'*

Stephen Westgarth (11)
Moorside Comprehensive School

ASSIST HER

I hadn't seen my daddy that night but when he burst through the door
I got quite a fright,
'It's a girl' were the words he said, as he picked me up and kissed
my head.

Everyone in the room began to go wild. It was too much for such
a small child.
'You've got a sister' is what I was told. But I'm only a year and nine
months old!

It's too early. This can't be. But sure enough it had happened to me.
I wanted my mammy so I started to cry. She didn't come running,
I don't know why.

It normally worked, where was she at? Then he put me in the car
and there I sat,
'til we reached a place where I'd never been, and there were lots of
people that I'd never seen.

He took my hand and led me towards a huge great building with
double doors.
Round a bend, she was here I'm certain, I knew for sure when he
pulled back the curtain.

There she lay on a big, bouncy bed. 'Hello Sweetheart,' she simply
said.
All of a sudden I heard a strange sound. Where was it coming from?
I looked around.

He picked me up so I could see, into the cot, a smaller version of me.
It had thick black hair and big blue eyes. As it screamed in my face,
I got quite a surprise.

'Say *'Hello'* darling, her name is Louise.'
'Can I hold her daddy, please?'
So onto my knee came this thing called a sister. I held her close and
then I kissed her.

Then my dad whispered in my ear so that I was the only one that
could hear.
'You must watch over her not just now, but forever. She'll be your
best friend so stick together.'
All of those months they had waited, to see if I would really hate it.
But I had to love her, she was like me but I could have done without
the responsibility
Of keeping her company when she was down and making her laugh
when she used to frown.
Watching over her when she was in trouble. Like a second shadow,
I had a double.

Wherever I went, whatever I did, standing behind me would be this kid.
And as we grew up to love one another I have to thank my father and
mother,

For giving me someone who'll always be there, when I'm feeling
lonely or in despair.
She owes me a lot and will repay me in time for the things she
wanted, just because they were mine.

Now and again we used to battle, every time I pinched her rattle.
But I knew from the second that I squeezed her that she was made
so that I could tease her.
Those ground rules that my dad had laid, were set in stone, to
be obeyed.

Michelle Donaghy (15)
Moorside Comprehensive School

GRANDMA

I went to my gran's every Sunday
and every week was the same.
I would be bored and couldn't wait until Monday
so I wouldn't have to go there again.

But Sundays always came round quickly
and so at my grandma's I sat.
The smell of her smoke was so sickly
but I just had to put up with that.

One morning I got a phone call
'We're going to see Newcastle train.'
My dad's friend was taking me to football
and told me to be ready straightaway.

I flew upstairs like a bat out of hell
and got ready as fast as I could.
I heard a small ringing of a bell
and listened, as in the porch my mum stood.

'Oh no!' I heard her frightened voice say
'I'll tell him straightaway.'
She went to my dad, 'I'm afraid your mum is dead
and your sister is on her way.'

I just sat down inside my room
her voice echoing in my head.
Tears streamed down my face
at the thought of mum saying, 'She's dead.'

For weeks and weeks I sat in my room
My personality? There was none.
My grandma, I missed so very much
I just couldn't believe she was gone.

I suppose what I'm saying now
is I realise I miss her a lot.
And if I could, I'd be bored every Sunday
I'd not argue, definitely not!

Amy Matthews (15)
Moorside Comprehensive School

THE KNIGHT AT SEA

The waves were as high as mountains,
As the storm raged on and on,
The fisherman struggled to control his craft,
As the seagulls cried their song.

The lightning flashed,
The thunder crashed,
The sea was as black as coal,
Could he get to port in time,
Before the end of day?

The port was in his sight,
The lighthouse light was bright,
The howling wind and pelting rain,
Could not deter this knight

The port was there within his reach,
The battle was nearly over,
The fisherman's job was almost done,
The storm had lost, the fisherman won.
He lived to fight another day.

Wayne Galloway (11)
Moorside Comprehensive School

HORSES AND PONIES

Galloping to and fro,
Never going fast, never going slow,
Taking it at their pace,
Waiting to have a galloping race,
Some just stand, others just gaze
Most of them, in a daytime daze.

Galloping to and fro,
Never going fast, never going slow,
Taking it at their pace,
Carrying people on their backs,
Riding out in the country for 'hacks'.
Giving them a wash, giving them a bath,
This is the time for a good old laugh.

Galloping to and fro,
Never going fast, never going slow,
Getting old and stiff,
Time to settle, have a foal,
Retire and have a dusty roll,
Watching foals gallop about,
Jumping over the old water-spout.

Galloping to and fro,
Never going fast, never going slow,
A new generation of horses and ponies,
And next year we'll see more,
Probably over the large stable door!

                                Neigh . . .

Jenna Ashton (12)
Moorside Comprehensive School

MR SPOT O'SAURUS

I am a spotty dino,
made of soft 'Fimo',
I like to eat spotted dick,
the bowl is nice to lick,
I like mum's custard,
followed by a tub of mustard,
I have yellow spots,
lots and lots and lots,
I have spikes on my back,
they'll never make a dino track,
I used to eat lime jelly,
I stopped because I had a fat belly,
I got poked in the eye,
it nearly made me die,
so don't be scared of me,
I couldn't hurt a flea.

Freya Claydon (12)
Moorside Comprehensive School

THE STORM

The thunder rattled across the plain,
Howling wind and lashing rain.
And then with an almighty crack,
The lightning struck the farmyard shack.
Soon the barn was well on fire,
And began to spread towards the byre.
The elements had done their share
Of bringing chaos and despair.

John Milburn (11)
Moorside Comprehensive School

THE STORM

The sky was blue,
But soon was grey.
The trees were still,
But began to sway.

Thunder roars,
Like a lion.
Faces at windows,
Some are crying.

Splish, splash, splish, splash
See the rain.
Splish, splash, splish, splash
Feel the rain.

Lightning flashes,
Thunder roars.
People running,
For indoors.

I wish the storm,
Would go away.
It spoiled,
A lovely summer's day.

The trees were still,
As still can be.
The sky is like,
A big calm sea.

Laura Farthing (11)
Moorside Comprehensive School

Storm

The storm is a giant, throwing flashes of yellow,
Angrily he roars and stamps, and stamps
His face like stone,
His teeth like razor-blades,
His hair like black clouds,
His eyes like lamps.

He flies like the wind,
As quick as a flash,
He puffs and pants,
Then his army of droplets go for a splash.

He roars even louder as the children cry,
Out comes the sun to make things dry,
The storm goes away with never a trace,
The storm will be back, he'll be there on
the case.

David Grix (11)
Moorside Comprehensive School

The Storm

The wind was howling like a beast,
The sky was as black as coal,
The wind came roaring from the east,
Which sent a shiver to the soul.

The rain lashed down like a wild whip,
When the lightning struck out,
The mist floated by, like a ship
When the leaves were dancing all about.

Abbie Whitehead (11)
Moorside Comprehensive School

Life's Unfair

For 12 years I had a gran,
Big and bold and smelt of 'old'.
To my dad she was a mam,
All her grandchildren, she would hold.

Illness took a hold of her,
Cancer was its name.
No longer could I hear her purr,
Just to be pain-free, was her aim.

Life was going in her eyes,
Like a dimming light.
The breaking of bonds of life ties,
Dog-tired, weary and worn, no fight.

No more happiness to give,
No black bullets, no hugs, no love left.
No will to live,
Just pain and anguish leaving me bereft.

Mother's Day came and went,
The last time I saw her face.
Her last breath, like a gentle wind spent,
Life's race lost, no matter the pace.

No last farewells were spoken,
We never said goodbye.
You were gone before I was woken,
Why cancer? I will never know why.

Sadness, anger, like black clouds,
Descended upon the loved ones.
Huddled together, covered in shroud,
The light switched off - gone.

The funeral day arrived,
I was dressed in black.
I cried and cried and cried,
Gone forever, to never get her back.

My memories I hold dear,
The smell, the softness, the love and care.
Like gentle rain a silent tear,
A feeling of being cheated - life's unfair.

Louise Roe (15)
Moorside Comprehensive School

TYRANNOSAURUS REX

The tyrannosaurus strode into the clearing,
Its leg muscles moving like well-oiled pistons,
It strode, covering ten feet with each step,
Causing miniature earthquakes whenever it put its
                                        feet down.

Its skin was armoured and scaly,
And covered with insects and creatures,
So that it moved even when it was still,
And crawled all the time.

Its head was a massive boulder,
A ton of sculptured stone,
And the teeth were needle-sharp daggers,
Arranged in a death grin.

The roar was that of a thousand lions,
Louder than a space-rocket,
Eardrum-bursting,
It could be heard a *million* miles away.

It towered like a skyscraper,
It could reach up and grab the moon,
Men were like mice to it,
It was the king of its time.

Adam Nash (13)
Moorside Comprehensive School

TYRANNOSAURUS REX

The T-Rex was big and tall
Its skin all pebbled like a wall.
Its boulder-stone eyes, white and round
Eckles was so scared, he fell to the ground
Its head looked like sculptured stone
A ton of ivory and bone
Big cage-like teeth, bigger than daggers
It gracefully runs and never staggers
Its tail so strong, it wiped out trees
It destroys anything it sees
And finally they shot it down
There was a big crash as it hit the ground.

Vicky Nash (12)
Moorside Comprehensive School

MYSELF

I am a dog,
    people's best friend.

I am Coca Cola,
    your favourite and the best.

I am a taxi,
    I'd be on time and never let you down.

I am a comfy seat,
    relax yourself with me.

I am some underwear,
    I'll support you when something goes wrong.

I am a cinema,
    have some fun and a good time with me.

Jon McClaren (13)
St Bede's School

AUNT ALICE

Evil aunt Alice with hair like snakes,
I really hate the smile she fakes.
She moans about her aching bones,
A look from her, could turn you to stone.

Oh evil aunt Alice, I hate you so!
With your wiry figure, why can't you go?
You sit there pretending you're really nice,
But I know that you enjoy eating mice.

Oh horrid aunt Alice, you are a witch.
To inflict me with pain, your nose, you twitch.
Your eyes reflect much destruction and death
To be quite honest, I prefer Aunt Beth!

Ben Elliott (12)
St Bede's School

HANNAH

A glossy coat with jet-black hair
Mysterious blinking eyes,
Approaching me with a gentle purr,
'Feed me' she cries.
Mewing, rubbing, purring persuasively
She begs,
I cannot walk, I cannot move,
She's twirling round my legs.
She'll get her way, she always does,
By putting on this play,
I'm sure it's only cupboard love
That leads to this display.

Michelle McMahon (13)
St Bede's School

People

Flesh and bone and smooth, coloured skin,
Hold a multitude of worlds within,
Feelings, thoughts and emotions too,
All come together to make an individual you,
Colours ranging from black through to white,
Those who see all, even when they've no sight,
Tall and strong, short and weak,
Most have tempers, others are meek,
Some are blessed with a special gift,
While others struggle, needing a lift,
Athletes, surgeons, philosophers too,
Who knows who'll be lucky? Me? You?
Cowards or heroes, who's to say,
What chooses our path or shows us the way?
Ours is a species for which there's no other,
Four titles each, girl, woman, wife and mother,
Boy, man, husband and dad,
Yet still another choice, good or bad?
One thing is as certain as the strongest steeple,
No matter the differences, we're all God's people.

Craig Davies (14)
St Bede's School

Not My Mum?

Not every child is special
In the same way as I
I have two mums
Don't ask me why.

I live with one
And don't know the other
I call one mum
And the other one, mother.

I have two brothers
Of whom I don't know
But when I am 18
To them I will go.

At first I didn't understand
But now I do
But for me
My love is split into two.

Katy McGeary (14)
St Bede's School

MATHEMATICS

Lying on the tangent of a circle that's too round,
Working out the route of a ship that's run aground.
Quadratic equations that are far too long,
Areas and angles that are probably wrong.

Protractors on the ready for our trigonometry,
Transformations are too hard for normal kids like you or me.
Loci and constructions, and polygons as well,
Rotating compound matrices are as difficult as hell.

Pythagoras' theorem, and someone else's law,
Who on earth they were, is all we want to know.
Prisms and pyramids, and shapes of every size.
Everyone in school must have heard our screams and cries.
Where's the point in maths?

Tracey Dixon (17)
St Bede's School

PLANES

Excitement, fear, happiness, nerves,
The feelings I feel, when I climb the steps,
At the top I meet the welcoming air hostess:
'Can I see your passport please?'
I flash my passport quickly at her
And enter the plane.
At first I feel claustrophobic
So I rush towards my window seat.

The engine rumbles . . .
And with a jolt, the plane accelerates down the runway.
Thrown back in my seat . . .
The plane takes off.
My ears pop when we reach the top.
I feel like a bird soaring above the clouds.

At that moment it is suddenly clear
I want to be a pilot for my future career!

Richard Peacock (14)
St Bede's School

THE SEA

An undecided flow of thought,
The shallow depressions
Eroding their habitat.
Serrations of hydrogen, oxygen,
Irritating the life.
Great storms of this
Repositioning its pavement.
Re-aligning its wake.

A searching grasp for time
A drowning soul, a limb.
As a paint brush
An attempt to colour,
Rearrange the air,
This fashioner of ladders
Imprinting the soft sky
With gentle patterns.

And so the riding torrents settle soon,
Creation, destruction,
A sculptor paralysed.
His brief art unrecognised.
This great colossus is not itself.
It is a mangler.
The absence of calm, a major role
The moon the actor.

But I, never victor, never reign
Destroyed, but as all to live again.

Stuart W Murray (12)
St Bede's School

Grandad

His thoughts, his loves, his cares, his way
They live with us, right here today
The way he gave his love to all
The way he walked, so straight and tall
That's the way he will always be
In memory looking back to you and me
He gave us strength and love and hope
And taught the lesson of how to cope
His apprehensions, disbeliefs and fears
He shrugged away throughout the years
So whether friend or family, show you care
He lives with us and will always be there
Be sad, unhappy, shed a tear
But don't worry, John's still here
So be happy, hopeful, for him, be glad
The friend, the grandfather the husband, the dad.

Steven Graham (16)
St Bede's School

Football

When the new season starts,
The stadium is alive.
As the players take the field,
Everyone cheers on their side.

As he flies down the wing,
His boots are ablaze.
You can hear the crowd sing,
As he leaves defenders in a daze.

When we meet a hard team,
Our hearts miss a beat.
We need the three points,
To turn up the heat.

To lose this match,
Would be too much to mention.
We are on our toes,
You can feel the tension.

The last match of the season,
We are as high as kites.
If we win this game,
We will be in the Champions' League by tonight.

Paul Walker (11)
St John's School

THE NIGHT

All dark and quiet
So black and scary
Mams and dads, boys and girls
Rested as can be
Trees rocking backwards and forwards
So soft and blowing in the wind
The street lights shining from above
Shining bright on the glittering houses
Shining on the wonderful trees
A cat shrieks in the darkness
Silence has gone
An owl in the distance hoots
A wolf cries
The milkman driving as bottles
clatter and rattle
The paper-boy comes stuffing
and squashing the papers through the letterbox
And then as the dawn breaks
The night has gone.

Michael Hartmann (11)
St John's School

COLOURS

Red is the colour of fresh ripe tomatoes,
Large and round like cricket balls.
Yellow, the shade of the sun in the sky,
Bright and glaring as the bulb of a lamp.
The blue of the sky is the colour of the sea,
With waves of clouds rolling by.
Sheets on the line, of a flaming pink,
Roar as they tangle in the wind.
The unripe banana, sits green in the bowl,
Waiting for sunlight, to improve the hue.
Thick grey fog, rolls over the hills,
Clearing slowly, in the dawn's early light.
Satsumas, mandarins, all orange in colour,
Small in size, but big in flavour.
Tree trunks of brown, stand upright and tall,
Initials engraved, who knows how old.
The bruise on my arm, purple as a plum,
Hurts if I touch it, but not for long.
Beige the colour of sandstone brick,
Surrounding a fire of flaming gas.
Colours they're bright, colours they're dull,
Where would we be if we were without them.

Richard Morley (11)
St John's School

AUTUMN DAYS

Autumn is a wonderful time,
With leaves of amazing colours like the paints on a pallette.
Leaves drifting gently to the hard dirty floor.
Trees losing their thick, bushy coating of leaves.
The melody of summer birds, as sweet as a group of pipers playing,
will soon be forgotten,
As the summer birds gather in trees to start their migration.
But the robins will soon be here, singing in the snowbound bushes.

In the evenings, the sun is setting.
The sunset is a perfect oil painting.
Early in the morning the air is misty.
On the grass lie perfect miniature crystal diamonds of dew.
From the trees, little conkers cascade.

The nights are getting dark.
The shadows of trees, and other objects sprawl around like creepers
up a wall.
Some days are very blustery,
Trees will sway from side to side.
With their long brittle fingers, sprouting all around.
As the days turn cold, squirrels and other animals prepare to hibernate.
You will not see them for the long cold winter.
If you are lucky you may see a fox or a rabbit darting across the road.
Faster than a speeding bullet.
By now people are huddling up, and preparing for the cold to come.

Adam Blenkinsop (11)
St John's School

The Hawk

The brown-stained hawk,
gliding swiftly through the air
over lush green treetops.
You find it resting in the countryside.

It hovers in the clear blue sky
like a helicopter waiting to land.
Below the innocent creatures
run wild with fear.
The cruel beady-eyed hawk
waits patiently for its hunted prey.

It swoops down upon it
puncturing the tensed skin
with its long sharp talons like daggers.
It soars high in the sky like an aircraft taking off,
dragging the inert animal
back up through the sky
to its camouflaged nest,
where starving young lie
waiting to be fed.

The hawk shares the innards of the dead animal
with its young,
preparing them
for the hard fight for survival
in the countryside.

Jake Farrell (11)
St John's School

A Day At The Seaside

I felt like a ride to Blackpool
One lovely summer's day
I sat upon the sands there
To watch the children play.

As I looked at the tower
And the old trams going by
I even saw the helicopter
Flying in the sky.

I went up in the tower
I could peer for miles around
The sea was a lovely shade of blue
I was a long way from the ground.

I'd been along the promenade
It was a long way out to sea
I didn't pay for anything
Everything on there was free.

I came down from the tower
It was nice to be safely back on the ground
I had a lovely afternoon tea
Then I was homeward-bound.

Carl McGregor (11)
St John's School

A Pride Of Lions

The pride lies on the African plain,
Waiting for their prey
The cubs fight in the tall yellow grass,
As little children play.

Their mothers with their darting eyes,
Searching for the food.
A father's mane glows in the sun,
As he carefully guards his brood.

A lioness, jumping up,
Spies an unsuspecting deer.
The chase is on, they run and run,
The lioness comes near.

The deer escapes into the bush,
Hunting was a chore.
The lioness is weary,
She can do no more.

The night approaches, the cubs will sleep,
Though their hunger brings them sorrow.
Their mother lies restless all night long,
Hoping they'll eat tomorrow.

Sarah McGough (11)
St John's School

The Farm

Down on the farm
It's an animal town
Cows are milking
In the barn.

Pigs in their sty
Rolling in the mud
Under the bright blue sky
Getting dirty as they should.

In the farmyard
Lives the sheepdog
Always on his guard
Giving warnings is his job.

Hens are pecking
At the ground
Eating any grain
They have found.

Sheep are grazing
In the fields
Little woolly lambs
At their mothers' heels.

In the yonder
As the water flows
Ducks on the pond
With their babies in tow.

Victoria Ratcliffe (11)
St John's School

WILD HORSES

Horses running wild and free,
Mares and foals for all to see.
Across rivers and hedges,
They run wild from anything they suspect.

As they gallop,
The wind thunders into their faces.
Eyes glare and nostrils flare,
Their coats gleam but don't like to be seen.

They whinny to each other,
Saying 'I am here.'
They look for their leader,
He must be here.
They come to a hill
And there they see,
The big black stallion bold and free.

He stands proud,
And looks after his crowd.
When danger he sees,
He will stand in the breeze
And call to his mares,
To run wild and free.

Gemma Bell (11)
St John's School

A DAY AT THE SEASIDE

I remember when I went to the seaside.
I went to Blackpool,
And I saw
Donkeys and people having donkey rides,
Children playing with buckets and spades
On the sand,
Children digging,
Building sandcastles.

Along the sea-front, a busy road.
A bit of drizzle,
A bit of sunshine.
On a fair May day,
Unattended cars lay
In car parks full.
Hotels lined up like dominoes
And people queuing for ice-creams.

Illuminations flashing along the promenade,
Youths playing in amusements,
Children buying candyfloss,
Hungry grown-ups buying fish and chips,
Kiddies paddling while their parents
Have a pleasant walk along the pier,
Screams from the big dipper
Howling in their ears.

And that is what I see
When I remember my day at the seaside.

Richard Simpson (11)
St John's School

ONE SUNNY DAY

One sunny day on a field behind a hill,
Lots of lovely flowers grew up
Straight and tall.
All the colours of the rainbow,
They grew and grew and grew.

There were little pink ones blowing in the wind.
Blue ones, purple ones, orange ones
And yellow ones grew up tall and proud,
Long ones, tall ones, short ones and small ones,
Growing together.

One sunny day something sad occurred.
A big ugly monster ploughed through the field.
As it ploughed through the field
You could hear its engine roaring.
Soon all the pretty colours had gone
And the field was plain and bare.

When the field was bare
The monster's job was done.
It rode off into the sunset.
One sunny day a field was plain and bare.

Katie Fowler (11)
St John's School

THE BIKE

It is bright red and shiny
As she takes me up the hill.
She zooms along the flat
As the wind blows in my face like a fan.

She has ten gears and headlights
And she is a brilliant bike.
She flies down the hill
As fast as a falcon.

She is the best bike ever.
Everyone else's bike is dirty
But my bike is lovely and clean.

She shines bright
As bright as the sun.
I used to have a green bike
But I didn't like that one.

My brothers try to ride her
But if they do I tell them off.
Then they get off
Because they might spoil her.

But three years later
I had to sell her
Because she was too small
But then I got another one.

Sara Elmes (11)
St John's School

NEW DAY IN THE OCEAN

The deep ocean glistens in the morning sun,
A beautiful day has just begun.
The tropical fishes begin to arise,
They stare around with wandering eyes.
In their large schools they playfully swim,
Hiding in the seaweed.

As the day goes on,
The giant sharks begin to stir.
They do not seem to be aware
Of the fish around them.
So off they swim in search of prey,
To begin the brand new day.

Now the ocean has come to life,
The coral is beginning to sway
In the soft, gentle touch of the waves.
The man-eating plants and the octopus are
Tucked away in the darkness,
Waiting for an unsuspecting victim
To unknowingly cross their path.

Whales have begun to move,
The majestic rulers of the waves.
Nobody dares approach them.
Mother fish pick up their babies,
In fear of their families being savaged
By the greatness of the whales.

The blue ocean dances merrily
With the afternoon breeze,
Morning has ended.

Hannah Daltry (11)
St John's School

The Great Ball Race

My ball fell out of the window and went
Boing, Boing, Boing.
Down the hill it bounced, going
Doing, Doing, Doing.
I started running after it at quite a pace
And people started joining the great ball race.
It bounced round the corner at the bottom of the street,
All you could hear was the sound of running feet.
Over the bridge it vanished, out of sight,
Everyone was running now with all their might.
Boing, Boing, Boing,
We could hear but could not see,
As it gathered up more speed, and headed for the sea.
Voices in the crowd were shouting 'Run, Run, Run,'
And all who'd joined the running, were having lots of fun.
But the ball just kept on bouncing,
It just did not want to stop.
It looked just like a rabbit,
Going *Hop, Hop, Hop.*
It was heading for the bottom,
Where the road becomes quite flat.
I must hurry, I must hurry,
Quite sure I was of that!
Boing, Boing, Boing.
When would it run out of steam?
I woke up in a sweat, had it all been a dream?
I turned to the window
And there on the sill,
Was my lovely bouncy ball
Which was absolutely still!

Penny Foster (11)
St John's School

NIGHT-MAIL TRAIN

Racing along the rusty line,
Trying to deliver the mail on time.
Through the valleys like a flash,
Always in a tremendous dash.
Throwing black smoke into the air,
Even if it's harmful she doesn't care.
Into Waverley ten minutes late,
Oh no, she's got to be at London at eight.
Down the line at Concorde speed,
Down through Newcastle and Berwick-upon-Tweed.
Winding through the beautiful countryside,
Through the large county of Humberside.
Passing herds of cows in the fields,
They annoy her but she never yields.
Approaching Mansfield station time to unload,
She's one minute late leaving and there's not far to go.
Whizzing through the darkest of tunnels,
It's not very light but she illuminates her funnels.
Arrives at London one minute to eight,
The people love her because she's never late.

Sean Kay (11)
St John's School

SHADOWS

I have a little shadow
That goes in and out with me
And what can be the use of him,
Is more than I can see.

He is very, very like me from the heels to the head,
The funniest thing about him
Is the way he wants to grow,
Not like proper children,
Which is always very slow.

For he sometimes shoots up taller than a rubber powerball
And he sometimes gets so little,
That there's none of him at all.

James Davy (11)
St John's School

THE AIR

I walked in the big noisy factory,
It was very busy. I sat on the brown plastic chair,
People were working then I heard
Bang, boom crackle.
It was a big black machine
I saw it eating the wood
And spitting it back out in different shapes.

The engine was sending out furry bags of smoke
I was nearly choking on the stuff,
People were choking and coughing,
Just like I was,
I thought in my mind carefully
Why do people come to work in this lonely factory,
When one day these machines will kill them?

I ran straight out of the big brown steel door
And smelt the beautiful fresh air in my lungs,
I looked to my left and in the distance I saw Blueforest Wood.
Men were taking trees down for this polluted factory,
Why do people have to spoil this beautiful world?
I thought in my mind.

Sonny Rockett (11)
St John's School

The Sea

The warm gaze from the sun above,
Brings life and beauty to the sea,
The blue and green waves make little
Fish shimmer in the light,
Soft yellow sand beneath my feet,
Tickling as the waves rush in and out.

Under the deep blue sea,
Multi-coloured fish dart about,
The long green sea-kelp
Like fields of corn
Sways in the tide,
Crabs try to hide in the rocks below,
When unfamiliar sounds come by.

Far out where the sea is calm and wide,
A large ship comes into view.
The sound of its loud horn disrupts the
Tranquillity
Of the deserted shore,
The powerful flourishing sea,
The feeling of the unknown that's out there,
In deep deep waters no man has ever dived,
In time we may see all the wonders of the sea.

Emma Barker (11)
St John's School

SEA

In the sparkling sea,
The waves crash and bang.
They whizz over the rocks
and soak me and nan.

The eagles singing,
Flying all around.
Catching fish,
and lying them on the ground.

Dolphins flipping and tossing,
Large white splashes they make.
Swirls flowing turning and tipping,
When they jump back into the lake.

Seals sitting on the rocks,
Don't they look proud.
Stroking their long black whiskers,
and singing out loud.

They slide into the sea,
Kicking like whales.
Flapping their fins,
and swirling their tails.

Casey Mangles (11)
St John's School

When Lights Have Gone Out

Night has come
Things go dark.
To get asleep I read a book
That makes me go to the land of dreams.
I dream about stars like marbles
And fairy tales which are happy.

Sometimes I don't fall asleep
I think of death and gruesome monsters
They keep me up all night long.

I also think of awesome things
Like bedroom changes and
Money-making theme park designs.
I think of terrible thoughts too
Like past deaths, earthquakes, stampedes
And earth-shaking tremors.

When I dream all those things
I wake up and read a humorous book.
If a book doesn't help I wake my mam
She tucks me in.

I fall asleep. A new day is wakening
Sun is rising and mist thickening
A new day waits for me.

Philip J Santana Smith (11)
St John's School

DIFFERENCES

All of us are different,
In so many ways,
We should live together in peace,
Instead of fighting over our differences.

Black as a blackboard or as white like a sheet,
Nobody should care what skin colour we have,
Underneath we're all the same.

Rich or poor should have no
effect on the way we look at people,
Money can't buy happiness.

Fat as a pig or thin as a twig,
Don't judge by what you see,
Treat everyone with respect,
And they will do the same.

When you see someone different,
Don't turn and walk away,
They are just the same as you or me.

If their nose is covered in spots,
Or their hands are as wrinkled as can be,
Just do what you were doing.

The message I am trying to get across to you,
Although we look different,
We are all the same in one way.

Robert Jones (11)
St John's School

Who Is It?

As we all file past it
This thing it looks hot
Its hairy appearance covers
We will never know what
This creature controls us
For an hour a day
If my parents could see it
I can't think what they'd say

It's told not to smoke
But we all know it will
If I saw it at night
I am sure it would kill
With eyes of red
And a mouth of saliva
Yes you have guessed it
It's our bus driver.

Christopher Ranson (11)
St Leonard's RC Comprehensive School

The Sun

The sky is blue
The sky is grey
Where had the sun gone today?
The children danced
The children played
I wish the sun could have stayed.

Sarah McCully (12)
St Leonard's RC Comprehensive School

BUS JOURNEY

S is for smokers - pointless I think
T is for time - the bus arrives late

L is for late - the one thing I hate
E is for exciting - I wish the bus was
O is for older pupils who boss you around
N is for neglect - the bus is full up
A is for arrival - Oh no! I've missed my stop
R is for rivals - as more people get on
D is for driver - the old, grumpy one
S is for school - I hate it, it's mad.

Michael Weetman (11)
St Leonard's RC Comprehensive School

MY FAVOURITE THING

My favourite thing would have to be the drums,
I *love* the crashes and the boom, boom, booms,
It's *fantastic* when the snare drum makes a crack,
It's *great* to give the cymbal a whopping big *whack!*

It's brilliant the way the floor tom goes bong,
It's fun to play along to a famous song,
I *like* the sound of the hi-hat, it goes tsshh,
Yes, that's right my favourite the drums.

Adam Sinclair (12)
St Leonard's RC Comprehensive School

OH NO!

We've got a test next lesson,
Revision? - I've forgotten.
17 minutes to the bell,
What to do? I feel rotten.

Why do teachers make us do
these awful tasks and tests?
We have them over and over again,
Oh why won't they give us a rest?

I wish we could give the teachers,
a test on fashion or fun.
I wonder what their reaction would be?
They'd probably scream and run!

Time is ticking by quickly,
Oh heck! Only four minutes to go!
Ask myself a predicted question,
The battle in 1066? - I don't know!

Oh no! There goes that stinking bell,
I feel like I'm going to choke!
Oh well, there's nothing I can do now,
I'll just have to go for broke!

Jennifer Hastings (14)
St Leonard's RC Comprehensive School

A BUS JOURNEY HOME

I'm right in the middle of a great big fuss,
Everyone wants to be first on the bus.
I've got piles of homework but it can wait,
I'm out of school and I feel really great.

We've boarded the bus and are raring to go,
Out of school and all the way home.
Laughing, chatting and playing with friends,
But we've reached my stop and the fun's at an end.

Joanna Jones (11)
St Leonard's RC Comprehensive School

HUNGER

Its dark eyes stared into the night,
Lit only by the fire light.
He slowly moved towards the prey,
He had hungered for all day.
He reached out with his scaly arm,
In total cold but perfect calm.
He grabbed his prey by her long black hair,
She screamed out in complete despair.
The riots had gone on all week,
A perfect time for him to seek,
The prey to fill his endless craving,
For food to stop his crazy raving.
And now he had it in his grasp,
His prey, some food at long, long last.
He threw her down onto the floor,
A glinting knife was all she saw.
Slowly he devoured her head to toe,
His hunger at least for now would go.
And then he walked into the night,
Lit only by the fire light.

Peter Burlinson (13)
St Leonard's RC Comprehensive School

My Bus Journey

The day all starts when you walk to the bus stop,
You wait just a little while and the bus arrives.
Now everyone pushes and shoves to get on,
I get crushed with all this.
Then we all sit down and we are on our way again.

On the way there it's all very quiet,
People just whisper if they have anything to say.
We just sit there looking out the window,
Just getting ready to face another day.

On the way back it's a different atmosphere.
Everyone's chatting to their friends, singing and laughing.
We all just can't wait to get home.
One or two at the back smoke a little too.
I don't like it, but what can you do?
Hooray! Hooray! We're at my stop,
I have waited so long now it's time to get off.

Catherine McKenna (11)
St Leonard's RC Comprehensive School

Hallowe'en

Hallowe'en comes but once a year,
Ghosts and ghoulish figures, gather now to scare.
Children chanting, 'Trick or treat,'
Waiting to collect their candy sweets.
Witches on broomsticks fill the sky,
Casting dark shadows on passers-by.
Fancy-dress parties by candlelight,
People waiting to get a *fright!*

Fiona Granlund (13)
St Leonard's RC Comprehensive School

I Wish It Was...

At the bus stop
We will wait
And wish the bus
Will be late.

I wish the day was over
I wish the day was over.

The bus slows down
I feel a frown
Spread across my face.

I wish it was Saturday
I wish it was Saturday.

As soon as I get
On the bus
My friends give me
A smile and cheer me up.

I wish it was holidays
I wish it was holidays.

The bus slows down
My friends and I
Put on a frown
Whoops! I've forgotten
My book
I wish I could
Get back on that bus.

Adelle Outhwaite (12)
St Leonard's RC Comprehensive School

My Bus Journey To School

I always catch my school bus at ten past eight,
I am always early, I just don't want to be late.
I want a seat by a window to look through and stare,
At the people outside with the funny old hair.

The bus clatters along at a steady old pace,
The driver's got glasses and a funny old face.
The seats are all dirty, the engine is so bad,
The bus is just knackered, it's all very sad.

From Monday to Friday I get on the bus,
To travel to school, I don't make much fuss.
But the weekends are great, no school, no hassle,
No catching the bus, plenty of fun and dazzle.

Peter Nichols (12)
St Leonard's RC Comprehensive School

Spring

Spring is for lambs so white,
for leaves on trees,
for buzzing bees,
and times which bring delight.

Spring is for trees which bear fruit,
for walks in the countryside,
for days by the seaside,
and chicks so minute.

Spring is for fields so green,
for flowers so colourful,
nothing's ever dull,
in the season of spring.

Abigail Duggan (13)
St Leonard's RC Comprehensive School

MY BUS JOURNEY

Off I trot to the bus stop
waiting in the cold for the bus to come
around the corner,
I can see it coming,
On I trot rummaging in my pocket
for my money.
'Morning driver,' I always say,
Then I sit down and I'm on my way.
Looking out the window wondering
what it's going to be like at school today.
On I sit wanting to be back home
tucked up in bed.
'Oh no!' I say,
Now it's my stop,
Time to get off, time to get off
as I pressed the stop button
off I trot
To face my dreaded day at school.

Gemma Hewitt (11)
St Leonard's RC Comprehensive School

HALF-PAST THREE!

Half-past three is the time of day,
You hear me shout hip hip hooray!
The bell does ring for one and all,
We grab our bags and run out the hall.
School is over, but just for today,
I'll be back tomorrow, if it's not Saturday.

Katy Moore (13)
St Leonard's RC Comprehensive School

THE DRIVER

The smell of rubber,
A boy's delight,
The British Grand Prix,
I've been travelling all night.

The flags are all waving,
The place is a-buzz,
That magical feeling,
Now I feel so good.

I look at my heroes,
They ready the car,
They soon accelerate,
They pull off afar.

They line up on the grid,
The fans spring alive,
The loudspeaker sounds,
The race starts in five.

The five mins pass quickly,
Our stomachs start rumbling,
The engines start roaring,
The commentator starts mumbling.

My driver made a great start,
First place he's gained,
He'll go on to win it,
If he only uses his brains.

He stood up on the rostrum,
He'd won it at last,
The nation all cheered,
His rival he'd passed.

So the driver returned,
The championship won,
We also went home,
The trip had been fun.

Simon Farthing (13)
St Leonard's RC Comprehensive School

A Normal Day At School

I walk into school what do I see?
Everyone around is staring at me.
I go up to Tutor without delay
I collect my planner from where it lay.
'Katrina,' Miss shouted 'Stay behind
I would like you to do a reading if you don't mind.'
Some of my teachers are okay
But it depends what lessons I've got today.
Today is Thursday as you know
What are my lessons today the poem will show.
I have PE and French And Tech as well
After dinner we have maths with 8L.
In PE we have to do gym.
In French I have to work with Tim.
Tomorrow we are having a party with 7N.
We have made friends with someone called Ben.
I've done my homework and it's a good job
Or I'd be on detention for Mr Thingymybob.
The bell's just gone it's half-past three.
On the bus I'll sit next to BB.
Whilst I'm at home I'll pack my bag.
It's school tomorrow oh what a drag.

Katrina Hesketh
St Leonard's RC Comprehensive School

HARTLEPOOL UNITED

Hartlepool United are my team,
When I see them play it's like a dream.
We've already beaten Torquay and Shrewsbury Town,
At our little stadium Victoria Ground.
But I've got my ticket I'm on my way,
To go and watch Hartlepool play.
And no one knows what the score will be,
Why, Cooper might score three.
The game's kicked off, we are underway,
We'll show Orient how to play.
Allan's scored, and we shout with glee,
'Hooray the Pool let's make it three.'
All the fans are celebrating including me,
When I know we've won, it makes me gleam.
I know Hartlepool are my team.

Ian Wilson (13)
St Leonard's RC Comprehensive School

MY BOYFRIEND

My boyfriend is handsome
My boyfriend is cute
My boyfriend is funny
In fact he's a hoot.
When we go out together
My friends always say
I suppose you're going to marry
That lovely lad one day.
I lie in my bed night after night
And think to myself
That he's my Mr Right!

Kelly Hewitt (11)
St Leonard's RC Comprehensive School

WAR

My name is Sergeant Lightning Flash,
I went to war with two big guns.
My secret name is Mr Mash,
The army's never much fun.

I drove a tank along the mud,
The lightning fluttered around.
When all the batteries then went dud,
We were left without a sound.

We went out and walked through the woods,
Crawling, quietly and still.
Guns were firing through sticky muds,
I thought 'Testament and Will.'

I fired the mortars, killed a man,
We ran and climbed up a tree.
Can I make it? Of course I can,
There's hope for my friends and me.

We climbed down and walked from the tree,
Everyone was almost dead.
I was left without injury,
'The war's over,' someone said.

We walked for miles and yet to find,
The body of my loved one.
The war had drove me, out my mind,
The sounds of war have not gone!

The war was futile, we had won,
Families were reunited.
Back to base camp, hand in my gun,
War hero? I was knighted!

Philip Curry (13)
St Leonard's RC Comprehensive School

THE COLD TOUCH

I left the dim lit boathouse,
Alone one autumn eve.
The shrill cry of tired birds,
Warned me of what I was to receive.

The moon hid very silently,
Behind the old church steeple.
The path I walked was long and lonely,
Far from friendly people.

I glanced nervously to my right,
There was something that craved my attention.
It was long, grey and frightful,
I had a sudden urge of temptation.

As I walked a little closer,
To see what lay behind,
The twisted long grey somethings,
A thought crept into my mind.

Long, grey and bony?
They could only be one thing.
Petrified I ran off,
My heart quickly thumping.

Fingers belonging to who?
A ghost, a vampire or a beast?
I wasn't going to wait to find out,
I'm sure I'd be a tasty feast.

I called for a taxi,
Told the driver where to go.
Soon I'd be home and safe,
But what was I to know?

He told me the price,
Of what I was to pay.
I reached to give him the money,
But his hands, on that seat I forever lay.

Katherine Rooke (14)
St Leonard's RC Comprehensive School

DEATH

I have a fear of death
Of dying all alone,
Without my family by my side
Unable to reach the phone.

What happens when we leave our bodies
Nobody does know,
Even though many have died and gone
What happens when we go?

My fear started weeks ago
When I lost a family soul,
I'm now scared to sleep at night
My family is no longer whole.

What's the point of life
When eventually we *all* die?
What's the point of taking away our families
When it only makes us cry?

When my mam was taken from me
I thought that there was no point of life,
But somehow she got sense to me
It would only cause my family *more* strife.

Caroline Marsh (13)
St Leonard's RC Comprehensive School

The Teacher

Getting up one morning,
She slithered out of bed.
Sliding down the banister,
To meet the day ahead.
Gone into the gardens,
To get her daily worms,
Placed them with baked beans,
Just think of all the germs.

Getting on her broomstick,
She makes her way to school,
Frightening all the children,
Looking like a fool.
She went into the classroom,
Scraped her nails down the board,
Thinking what to do next,
She got out her sword.

Help! Screamed the children,
As she threw it through the desk.
'Well now children,'
'Here is a test.'
Screaming as they ran outside,
Through the gate, along the path.
'Will you last another day?'
She said, as she laughed.

Sarah Williams (12)
St Leonard's RC Comprehensive School

WAR

Tanks firing here and there
Soldiers running everywhere
With the growing knowledge of death
They knew this could be their last breath.

Air strikes launched
The enemy's glory flaunched
They felt that death was the only option
As they lay there, frightened, watching.

Would they live, would they die
As they lay there pondering, why?
Wishing, hoping it would all end
But knowing their country they had to defend.

Guns not firing, must be jammed
Enemy's base, towering grand
Bodies strewn across the floor
We know this as death, they know it as war.

Philip Belton (13)
St Leonard's RC Comprehensive School

HOMEWORK

Sitting at home watching TV,
Feeling as happy as can be.
Oh no I feel such a jerk,
I've forgotten to do my homework.
Maths, history, science too,
Adolph Hitler? What? Who?
All this homework never ends,
I think I'm going around the bend.

Helen Campbell (11)
St Leonard's RC Comprehensive School

DOLPHIN POEM

It's a free and friendly animal
that can swim through the water all day.
It's an independent mammal that just
goes on its way.

Its face is a smiling picture
a friendly glorious sight.
It glides and jumps through the water
reaching a tremendous height.

They live on fish and squid
but would not harm you or me.
They are gentle harmless creatures
They are a staggering sight to see.

Laura Young (11)
St Leonard's RC Comprehensive School

SMOKEY

My budgie, my budgie,
My budgie was called Smokey,
Bright blues and greens,
He came down to share my dinner,
And ate some baked beans,
He shared my mashed potato,
And drank my lemonade,
But he never had toast without his marmalade.

My budgie, my budgie,
He squawked with delight
And when you said hello,
He was ever so polite.

My budgie, my budgie,
He gave us a fright,
For poor little Smokey had died in the night.

Lydia Davison (12)
St Leonard's RC Comprehensive School

MY BUS JOURNEY

To the front of the queue I'm rushing,
But it's hard because everyone's pushing.
At last I'm on the bus,
Still people are making a fuss
And the ones coming on are gushing.

As the bus moves on and on,
Half the people have gone.
Still loads of people are talking,
As we pass a few poor people walking
And we trundle on and on.

Hey, look! Now it's my stop,
When I ring the bell off I'll pop.
I'll wave bye to my friend,
As the bus goes round the bend
And then I'll go to the shop.

Helen Jones (11)
St Leonard's RC Comprehensive School

THE BUS JOURNEY

It's twenty past eight,
I'm running late.
I'll miss the bus to school.

Down the road,
With my heavy load.
I'll be late for school.

Into the shop, for a can of pop,
Then I hurry out to the bus stop.
Will I be late for school?

At the queue I wait and wait,
While others mutter the bus is late.
We'll all be late for school.

The bus arrives, we all chatter,
We ask the driver, *'You're late. What's the matter?'*
We can't be late for school.

The driver's sick, I think he's choking,
It must be from all that horrid smoking.
We will be late for school!

Sarah Oliver (11)
St Leonard's RC Comprehensive School

COMPUTER

Our school has a computer
He thinks he's oh so good
But sometimes he's not brainy
Like his head was made of wood

He has a big wide screen
With a little mouse and pad
With letters on the keyboard
That sometimes drive you mad.

Cheryl Wright (11)
St Leonard's RC Comprehensive School

THAT FRIDAY NIGHT FEELING

It's that Friday night feeling
And a quiet relief flows over the bus
And lulls us all half to sleep.
The movement of the bus,
Sad songs on the radio,
The quiet buzz of chatter,
The feeling just flows.

It's that Friday night feeling,
The weekend's ahead,
It'll be ten o'clock tomorrow
And you'll still be in bed.
Sleepovers, parties,
Excitement's on its way,
But it's all calm and quiet,
This time today.

The bus comes to a stop,
There's a rush to get off.
It's hectic again,
It's getting pretty rough.
That Friday night feeling is over and gone,
But next Friday's bus ride there'll be another one.

Laura O'Hagan (11)
St Leonard's RC Comprehensive School

THE ROWER

I am a rower,
I row all day long
And if you pause for a moment,
I'll sing to you my song.

I row on a Sunday morning,
Once I've been to the swimming pool
And also on weekday nights,
Right after I finish school.

I mainly row in quads or doubles,
But sometimes I scull alone,
Although in the winter when it's cold,
I get chilled right to the bone.

Next year when I go to the Nationals,
I hope to strike Gold,
But that'll take a lot of training,
Or so I've been told.

Maybe when I'm older,
I'll make the GB squad,
Rowing in a coxless four,
Or perhaps a quad.

Well that's the end of my story,
So remember, even if you forget the rest,
That when it comes to rowing,
Leonard's are the best!

Paul Brady (13)
St Leonard's RC Comprehensive School

THE BUS JOURNEY

On our bus it's very quiet
Until night when it's a complete riot
Everyone's noisy and having fun
Because the school day's over well until tomorrow
The morning is boring
Nobody's noisy
I suppose it's because
There's a school day ahead
Or because everyone's half dead
Just like me
They've just climbed out of bed
Our bus drivers are nice
And they play some good music
We get stuck in the traffic
But we all don't care
We're too sleepy to notice.

Rebecca Roche-Smith (11)
St Leonard's RC Comprehensive School

I WONDER WHY

I wonder why light's so bright,
And why we can never see at night.
Who told the animals to build their homes,
And taught us to brush our hair with combs?
Oh when the Earth was thought not to be round,
Where were the edges to be found?
Who lights the stars and paints the moon
Always on time never soon?
Who will tell me,
I know not who,
      Perhaps it's you?

Jonathan McIntosh (15)
St Leonard's RC Comprehensive School

WITH ONE KISS

Your eyes, like dew-blessed flowers
Still gaze
Past miles of unknown
Days of indifference, people, excitement, frenzy
Life.

Silver petals, floating on a tragic sea
Bridge two uncertain shores
Longing
Longing for answers
Longing for more.

Hushing leaves, willed by a tender breeze
Brush against my moistened cheek
Brush away the helpless tears
Brush away the hopelessness
Whispering that you love me.

Pierced by the bright darkness
Forced to surrender
Imprisoned in sleep;
Pushed through the abyss
Into your heart

With one kiss.

Lucy Glover (16)
St Leonard's RC Comprehensive School

MUD

M ucky, marvellous, mushy *mud*
U gly, unsightly, unusual *mud*
D irty, dull, delightful *mud.*

Catherine Hughes (12)
St Leonard's RC Comprehensive School

WHAT IS OUT THERE?

Something lies deep in the wood.
My curiosity leads me.
If only, if only, if only, I could
See what the creature could be.

I sense a feeling of death.
Everything is silent and still.
I crouched down among the heath
Waiting for the creature to make a kill.

I walked eagerly to where my soul guided me.
What the creature was I just could not see.
I was that frightened I felt paralysed, but was not alone
And I felt like I was entering a danger zone.

As I approached closer to the creature
I noticed a very distinctive feature.
Its eyes were as red as a flame
And started walking towards me looking very lame.

The shadows were very sinister as it fell midnight
And then I got a shocking fright.
It darted towards me from behind the trees
And by this sudden movement I fell to my knees.

I had a quick glimpse of the shadowy figure.
The trees had obstructed my view.
As it sprinted past me it gave a loud snigger.
The figure was almost see-through.

I still don't know what the figure was to this day
And no one believes me in what I say.

Joy Hewitson (13)
St Leonard's RC Comprehensive School

LIFE'S NOT FAIR!

Me: 'It's not fair!
Life's not fair!
I'm not allowed to do anything
It's just not fair!'

        Mum: 'You haven't done your homework.
                You said you'd clean the car.
                You're really too young anyway.
                It's just not safe . . . so there!'

Me: 'But Mum . . . all my friends are going!
They'll think I'm just a geek,
Their mums don't keep on nagging,
They go there every week.'

        Mum: 'I know you think I'm fussing,
                I know you don't understand,
                But one day you'll be a parent,
                And you'll know why you were banned.'

Me: 'I don't know why you worry,
You treat me like a child
You're really just a hypocrite
'Cos, Gran says you were *wild!*'

        Mum: 'I'm not prepared to argue,
                I'm not about to fight,
                I'm not your best friend's mother,
                I'm yours, so you're not going tonight!'

Me: You'd think I was going drinking,
Or out with girls all night,
It's only bungee jumping
That's making Mum uptight!'

Daniel Van Leempoel (15)
St Leonard's RC Comprehensive School

TV

Bored, zonked
Click - on it goes
Bright colours flash every second.
Booming noises in my head
Swamping me
Invading the living room.
Drowning me, brain dead
Zombified, staring
Jumbled up noises and pictures
Time-consuming
Goes on forever
Never ending, all night all day.
Bags growing under my eyes
Fixed, absorbed
Addictive TV.

Samantha Sheen (16)
St Leonard's RC Comprehensive School

COLUMBUS

In fourteen hundred and ninety-two
Columbus sailed the ocean blue.
He sailed with a crew
On a boat that was new.
He sailed to Asia to look for gold,
To make this trip he must have been bold.
He landed at last upon some sand
Hispaniola he called this land.
The Indians gave him a mask of gold,
He took it home so it could be sold.
He sold it for one hundred coins of gold,
By now Columbus was getting old.

Stephanie Nicholson (14)
St Leonard's RC Comprehensive School

STRESS IS . . .

Arranging a lesson
For an eighth year class,
All to get
An A-level pass.

Getting ready
There is no time,
Why did I do it?
It's such a bind.

Into the classroom
Already late,
The children are sitting
Awaiting their fate.

Set them to work
Just don't worry,
Now it's begun
I'm quite merry.

As quick as a flash
The lesson's over,
Something to do with
My four-leafed clover?

They file out of class
Not bad I guess.
That's my idea
Of classroom stress.

Marie-Claire Coxon (16)
St Leonard's RC Comprehensive School

IT WASN'T ME!

I trapped my brother's finger in the door.
My mother took my brother to hospital in the car.
Blood on the seat, blood on the door.
My dad's shadow crept over me 'Get to your room now!'

I trapped my brother's finger in the door.
It wasn't my fault, he shouldn't have had his finger in the door!
I didn't trap my brother's finger in the door.
He put his finger in the door.

It wasn't my fault.
It wasn't me.
It was him.
Honest!

Ian Mullany (15)
St Leonard's RC Comprehensive School

MY MAM

Nag, nag, nag
That's all she seems to do
Always moaning always twisting
That's all she seems to do.

Clean your bedroom, make your bed
That's all she seems to say
Do your homework go to bed
That's all she seems to say.

Washing, ironing and making meals
That's all she seems to do
Loving me and caring for me
That's why I love my Mam too.

Christopher Dodds (12)
St Leonard's RC Comprehensive School

INNOCENT!

When I was seven everything I did was bad
I was always getting wrong off Dad.
This day was no different
I got the blame
For smashing the greenhouse window pane.
'I'm innocent,' I shouted
'Go to your room and think about it.'
I got the blame
It was always the same.
Later on when things calmed down
In walked my neighbour with a frown.
He confessed his face was pale
He had come to tell his tale.
He was responsible for the window breakage
I was innocent, I didn't have to replace it.
My face lit up with delight
Dad was wrong and I was right.
Double pocket money for you
That was a change, out of the blue!

Tony Hutchinson (15)
St Leonard's RC Comprehensive School

HARSH WORDS

It was one cold winter's afternoon,
I was waiting for my bus.
I hoped the bus would come soon,
But it didn't, and I played.

I threw a snowball at my mate,
Not knowing what anger it would create.
I just wanted a bit of fun,
Blind to what was soon to come.

The head teacher put his hand on my shoulder,
His harsh worlds hit me like a boulder.
He told me to see him in his room,
Suddenly I filled inside with gloom.

I walked anxiously along the corridor,
My feet stuck to the floor.
I picked up litter for a day,
I was wrong and made to pay.

James Hicken (14)
St Leonard's RC Comprehensive School

Gossip, Gossip

It's all around the playground
And in the classrooms too.
Isn't gossip brilliant?
Not when it's about you.

When you fancy someone
You'll tell a friend or two.
At breaktime they'll tell a few
By lunch the joke's on you.

Joe's got a sprained ankle
Joe's got a broken leg
Joe got run over at the weekend
Did you know Joe was dead?

Everyone will gossip
Gossip is a part of life.
I gossip and so do you
It's always better to add on a thing or two.

Sarah Bailey (15)
St Leonard's RC Comprehensive School

COPYING

Last lesson on a Thursday
Miss Graham for our music time
All projects were handed back
Except for Laura's and mine

I got accused of copying
So I took the blame
When really it was Laura
Who had ruined my name

I got shouted at
And made to feel small
When it should have been Laura
Not me after all

I went red with anger
We had the class's attention
I got more homework
And a detention

Just I got wrong
'Cause I took the blame
When really it was Laura
Who had ruined my name

Laura got nothing
Not a detention
No extra homework
Not any attention.

Cheryl Murphy (14)
St Leonard's RC Comprehensive School

IT'S SO UNFAIR

One happy Friday morning,
another usual day at school,
was the one particular day,
that I was made out a fool.

It all started at ten past ten,
when me and my friend had a fight.
I was just pretending, but she was not,
so you can imagine it didn't turn out right.

She told all of our friends
that I had been a pain,
that I'd been a bully
and that I was the one to blame.

So I got wrong
and she did not.
She gave her story,
but made up the lot.

Now all of my friends,
they believed her story, which she had overtold,
that I was nasty, cruel and ghastly
and that she was as good as gold.

It was so unfair,
that I'd been treated in a horrible, untrue way
because I hardly caused a thing
that happened, on that supposedly happy day.

Natalie Wildish (14)
St Leonard's RC Comprehensive School

BLAMED

When I was at school
I brought a ball.
It smashed the window
              of the hall.

I got told off,
I was sad.
But the very next day,
I was really mad!

It wasn't my fault,
I got the blame.
My friend, the guilty,
Hung his head in shame.

Jonathan Stevenson (14)
St Leonard's RC Comprehensive School

THE TEST

Working hard for the
Geography test,
Sitting next to my
Best friend.

Thinking I had
Done so well,
Finding out I hadn't
Done so well.

Staying behind after
Lesson knowing Nicola
Had copied off me,
I couldn't believe her.

Teacher gives us
Extra homework,
Nicola has never
Been my friend since.

Emma Hann (14)
St Leonard's RC Comprehensive School

PERFECT MAN

As I looked at him,
A tingle passed down my spine.
His lovely blond hair,
His big blue eyes,
His smart dress-sense,
The chain around his neck.
Everything about him was perfect,
Nothing could be better.
Then I thought, 'If only I could have him,
If only I could get to know him.'
I thought of his voice,
It made the hairs on my neck stand on end.
I could picture him talking to me,
Laughing with me, holding my hand.
Pity it's just a fantasy,
I mean, it's only a picture in a magazine.

Lisa Richardson (14)
St Leonard's RC Comprehensive School

REALLY

Lying in bed,
Feeling really ill,
Really can't move,
Really have to lie still.

Lying in bed,
Really want to cry,
Really can't move,
Feels like I want to die.

Lying in bed,
My head is really thumping,
Really can't move,
My heart is really bumping.

Lying in bed,
Doctor comes to see,
Really can't move,
He's frowning over me.

Lying in bed,
Bro comes in to laugh,
Really can't move,
Really need a bath.

Lying in bed,
No one's hand to hold,
Really can't move,
But all I've got's a cold!

Helena Jackson (15)
St Leonard's RC Comprehensive School

THE AFRICAN PLAINS

As I walk through the long, spiky grass,
I watch my prey as they twitch with anticipation,
The small insects of the hot African flatlands,
Spring and hop trying desperately to find a cool spot,
In the far distance I can sense a killing of an antelope,
I ask myself if I should join in with the feasting,
I stop and ponder on the thought for a minute or two,
I quickly decide to stay and get a full antelope to myself,
The heat teems down on me as I wander around my prey,
In a strange sort of way I feel sorry for these animals,
But life must go on,
And lions will always kill antelope.
The antelope kill mice and other little mammals,
And the mice kill worms and insects.
It's a way of life,
And if one of us break this chain we will all die of starvation.
The animals are tired and I can't waste any time.
I circle them and choose the best one,
Silence.
I pounce quickly,
The antelope scatter,
I grab and pick out the one I want,
I got it.
The lions strike again,
Blood spurts out and all that is left of that antelope is
A red stain on the floor of the African plains.

Jessica Eddie (13)
St Leonard's RC Comprehensive School

Love At First Bite

As my eyes meet his,
Delight fills my head.
The creaminess of his skin,
Makes me feel funny within.
He's sitting over there,
Tall, dark and lush.
Not a moment of despair
As I walk over there.
He's rolling in my mouth,
What a lovely sensation.
We must take things slowly,
I must be patient.
Unless I'll be lonely,
Without him beside me.
Milky, smooth and creamy,
Chocolate Alabama cake.

Lianne Crosby (14)
St Leonard's RC Comprehensive School

What Is A Million?

The blades of grass, growing on the lawn.
The people I've met since the day I was born.

The grains of sand found on the beach.
The age of a fossil, deep beneath my feet.

The years it would take to reach the sun.
The foods that I have eaten yum, yum, yum!

The water droplets that fill up the sea.
The words that I've read since I started to read.

The bright stars I see at night, twinkle, twinkle,
God bless sleep tight,
And I dream of a million dreams that
I dream tonight.

James Mallen (14)
St Leonard's RC Comprehensive School

COOL CLIMATE

I am a panda.
I live in the bamboo shoots,
Watching the sun slowly rise
Clearly on the mountainside.
I stand up lazily and look around.
The breeze hits the trees,
While the crisp leaves rustle.
I sit around,
Eating bamboo all day,
And watching the day go by.
As the people from Mount Fuji,
The people come and go,
Through the high hills and low valleys.
I pull the white roots and dream,
Looking at the seasoned trees in the distance.

Robert Paton (13)
St Leonard's RC Comprehensive School

SLEEPY PUPPY!

I sit in my warm basket,
Happy and content.
My ravenous appetite now satisfied,
I prepare myself for a sleep.

What's that, buzzing near my ear?
I lift my sleepy head,
And see a fly buzzing around the room.
Oh, I just wish it would let me sleep!

Well I'm awake now,
I'll never get back to sleep.
That fly just had to spoil my sleep,
Why won't it just mind its own business?

I'm going to catch that fly,
No matter what it takes,
Otherwise it will drive me mad!
Why won't it just stop that buzzing?

I lift my dainty paw,
Take a swipe at the fly on the window,
Take my paw off the window.
Oh, I missed it, fly, stop buzzing!

I know, I'll chase it!
I bound around the room,
In long strenuous strides,
Without any success, the fly still buzzes around!

Oh, I've had enough, I'm tired now.
I sit in my warm basket,
Watching the fly buzzing around the room.
All of a sudden, it disappears, where has it gone?
I look around the room,
Then a spider's web catches my eye.
The fly is stuck,
Peace at last!

Ruth Elder (12)
St Leonard's RC Comprehensive School

SCHOOL

Half-past eight,
He just woke up,
Late for school,
He missed the bus
Out the door
He's running late,
Resting on his shoulder
A bag of two tonnes weight,
Round the streets,
And on the run,
He reaches school,
The bell has gone,
Tuck that shirt in!
Blazer's on!
Hurry up!
The bell has gone!

Clare Puddifoot (12)
St Leonard's RC Comprehensive School

SLUDGE!

Sticky, sludgy, slippery, slime,
The ploppy, sloppy, creepy kind.
Slime in my pocket, in my shoe,
Is it custard, or is it glue?
Maybe it's lurking in the loo,
Careful it could pounce on you!
All this slime was admired and seen
By horrible things, yellow and green.
Slimy green things straight from Mars,
And planets far beyond the stars.
Fat, small, tall and lean,
Don't touch it, you don't know where it's been.
I'm glad that you are all my dream!

Katy Jennings (12)
St Leonard's RC Comprehensive School

COUNTDOWN TO MATCH DAY

Saturday morning 9am,
wake up excited, it's match day again.
Keep myself busy at least till noon,
then I get ready to watch the *Toon*.
1.30 comes and off I go,
hoping to see a 3-nil show.
It's now 2.30 the ground is lifting,
with all the noise the fans are making.
3 o'clock's here it's kick-off time,
whistle blows we're on our way
to yet another great *match day*.

Tom Marley (12)
St Leonard's RC Comprehensive School

Our Car Broke Down

The car broke down the other day
The wheels fell off and rolled away
The bonnet sprung open
The engine fell out
We tried to persuade Dad not to shout.

All of a sudden up the seat sprang
Our heads went through the roof *bang!*
Three holes in the roof
No engine, no wheels
All of a sudden there was a loud squeal
The kids and the Mum were not very happy
'Cause the little one had just wet its nappy.

Dad went for a walk to find a phone
And left Mum and the kids all alone
By this time it was very late
All of the food had been ate.

We rang the AA they arrived the next day
And towed us all the way home
But another holiday was yet to come.

We played and splashed all week long
It was good and it was fun
On the way back from our holiday
We were yet again in dismay
The car broke down again.

Annalise Simpson (12)
St Leonard's RC Comprehensive School

BLINKO THE ALIEN

2,000,000 miles away in outer space,
There lives an alien with an ugly face.
He's the most disgusting alien for miles around,
When he eats he makes a most disturbing sound.
His nose is purple and his ears are slime green.
When he is noticed people really *scream!*

With his forty eyes he can see,
Upwards and downwards and diagonally.
So trying to escape from him is not an easy task,
So please do not disturb him, do I really need ask?
If you are caught and squeal,
It won't help you, you're still his next meal!

2,000,000 miles away in outer space,
There lives an alien with a most disturbing face,
If you ever go up there and plan to stay alive,
Please don't go near Blinko, if you want to survive,
Lastly, if you see Blinko your life may be done,
Oh, and of course don't forget to *run!*

Marie Ford (12)
St Leonard's RC Comprehensive School

ANIMALS

Some are thin and slither like slime
Some are fat and roll in the grime
Some are ugly and snarl and snap
Some are cute yet nip and yap
Some live in water, swim and dive
Some live on land and don't need much to survive.
All animals are different in shape and size
But all are loveable and most are wise.

Ellena Plumb (12)
St Leonard's RC Comprehensive School

MY SISTER

My sister is a face I recognise but do not know
The owner of a red toothbrush
A lover of music, but I don't know what band
She owns the room next to me
She is music and she calls me deaf
She is water dripping away
That wants to hold before it is gone
She is a stranger I am longing to meet
But whom I fear I never shall
I am a box she does not want to open
I am a prayer she does not want to answer
Will not answer, cannot answer
I am a sand-timer running out of time.

Rachel Chadwick (12)
St Leonard's RC Comprehensive School

SUMMER

Summer is a season full of happiness and fun
As the children and the grown-ups go out into the sun.
The beaches are crowded
People getting tanned,
All around is happiness, joyfulness and fun.
People getting sun-tanned free of cares
As they lie on their red and yellow deckchairs.
Children eating ice-creams as they melt in the hot sun.
People shouting as they run.
Summer has come!

Elizabeth Powell (12)
St Leonard's RC Comprehensive School

ALIVE?

I wish I was alive
truly alive, to speak, to sing
to dance with the energy of
someone who is alive.
I wish one day to wake up
to the world and find myself awake.
Truly awake, to hear and smell
with the freshness of someone
who is awake.
I wish I felt no pain.
I wish each day would pass
without hateful words and painful thoughts.
I wish I felt nothing,
and could live each day in peace
to live before I die
and be alive.

Rachel Hooper (16)
St Leonard's RC Comprehensive School

A POEM ABOUT POEMS

P eople talking nonsense, don't understand these gibberish words.
O ld words, modern words, Geordy words, old English words,
   Scottish words, Welsh words.
E nglish, writing poems, haikus, acrostics.
M ake no sense to me.
S tupid things, who needs them.

    Poems!

Sean Morris (12)
St Leonard's RC Comprehensive School

DRINKER

My Father went to the pub one night,
And had a drink or two.
On his way home he got in a fight,
And a knife went through his shoe.

On the next day, he went again,
And bought a drink for his mate,
But when he got home he went insane,
'Cause his head got smashed on a gate.

My Father he went to the pub with Nick,
And had a drink or two,
But when he went to the toilet to be sick,
His head got stuck in too.

The next morning when he got up,
My Father's neck was sore.
The next step he took he tripped on a cup,
And his head went through the door.

Richard Lyons (12)
St Leonard's RC Comprehensive School

JUNK FOOD

I have to admit I'm a junk food nut
I eat junk food an awful lot
I eat chocolate, I eat sweets
I eat ice-cream and treacle treats
But my Mother does not approve
So my junk food is on the move
Where can I stash it?
Where can it go?
Sorry people I just don't know.

Eleanor Byrne (12)
St Leonard's RC Comprehensive School

School

If I didn't have to,
I wouldn't come to school,
I'd rather be on holiday,
Lying by a pool.

You're always getting homework,
You're always getting wrong,
When you're in your music lesson,
They make you sing a song.

You're always waiting ages,
For the holidays to come,
The teachers think they're clever,
But they really are dumb.

Kim Coates (13)
St Leonard's RC Comprehensive School

Life

Life,
What is life?
Something that passes us by day after day?
Something we struggle to earn?
Something we earn when we are born?
Nobody knows where life comes from.
Nobody knows what life is really all about.
Nothing can replace life.
So, what is life?
Life is forever!

Jill Richardson (16)
St Leonard's RC Comprehensive School

OAPs

Down at the Post Office every Monday morning!
Dull to listen to, incredibly boring!
Things were always better 'when I was a lad',
But these days the world is ever so bad!

They do have their good sides,
Paying you on theme park rides,
Shoving sweets down your neck,
Telling you how the world is such a wreck!

They're always complaining about children and school,
Saying, 'Things were never so easy when I went to school'
Enough of all this educational lark,
They all have dogs that can't help but bark!

I know I'm being horrible, awful at that,
But I'm very glad we had this chat,
It had to be admitted, the truth came out,
But don't tell them I said this or they'd probably shout!

Paul Edis (12)
St Leonard's RC Comprehensive School

CREEPY CRAWLIES

Creepy crawlies are so weird,
Hairy legs like a bushy beard.
Scorpions sting some can *hisss*.
Wings to fly through the sky,
Live a few days then,
Die.

Steven Howe (12)
St Leonard's RC Comprehensive School

MOTORBIKES

Turn the key rev it up
It should start up if you have any luck.

Hondas, Yamahas and Suzukis too
It is better riding one than having the flu.

50cc, 200cc it makes a big difference
200's are better and cover more distance.

Big ones, small ones, none are slow
You'll pay the price if you really want to go.

Big ones, small ones take your pick
It all depends if you can take the stick.

Scramblers go on dirt
But might muck up your shirt.

It doesn't really matter because they are worth the money
If you fall off it also might be funny, just as long as you don't hurt your tummy.

That's motorbikes.

Warren Kennick (12)
St Leonard's RC Comprehensive School

DRACULA

There once was a man called Dracula
He thought he was very spectacular
He liked to drink people's blood
People didn't think that he should
The fact that he killed for a living
Made people rather unforgiving

He would prowl about by night
Making sure he kept out of sight
He could turn into all shapes and sizes
From a bat to mist when the sun rises
He would stay in his coffin all day
But at night he would get his own way.

Stacey Denton (16)
St Leonard's RC Comprehensive School

THROUGH THE EYES OF A RODENT

I lie in a cage
A cage made as a home for me.
The cold of the bars is my torment,
The pain of my capture itself.
They refuse to give way to my gnawing,
My mouth is cracked and red.
The food they give me
The bedding they lay for me,
Unnatural.

The chance of my escape is nigh.
The door from my misery opens.
A gap in the bars of my prison
An opportunity to make haste and fly.
Yet alas my suffering does not end.
The claws of my captors are caring,
And they hoist me like an invalid
Caress me in their palm.
Place me in a sphere
And take amusement in my pain
For they know that I am meek.

Philip Morris (13)
St Leonard's RC Comprehensive School

FRIENDS

At night I dream of my friends,
And wish that I was there,
I know that they miss me,
But no one seems to care.

I want to be there back with them,
And be there as a friend,
I know that they'd protect me,
And I wouldn't go out like a trend!

At night I cry myself to sleep,
At day I think of them,
Oh why, oh why can't I go back?
I just want to have some friends.

Claire Gray (13)
St Leonard's RC Comprehensive School

CARS

Cars are fast shiny and bright
you will always see them in the daylight
some are fast and some are slow
it doesn't matter they all go.

Police cars shock you in the night
with their blue flashing light
hair goes up faces go white
and it all ends in the night.

Citroens
Audi
Rover
Skoda.

Daniel McCaffery (12)
St Leonard's RC Comprehensive School

The Lion's Mane

Majestic, noble,
I am Lord of all,
King of beasts,
Overseer of all I survey.

This is the pride land,
My pride land is the earth,
I rule the earth,
My mane is a symbol of power,
A figurehead for all.

I am the leader,
Born with royal blood,
I am the true beast,
The high beast!

I am not opposed,
Others are strong,
I am stronger,
Others are great,
I am greater.

My mane is the world,
The world is my court,
I am the King!

Long live the King!

Richard Villis (12)
St Leonard's RC Comprehensive School

DANNY BOY RIP

A visitor of his ancestors' abode,
Killed by hate on a road,
And now he's dead as dead can be,
He wins his killer's sympathy.

As both sides deny their blame,
The country has to share the shame,
And as the flowers rot on his grave
They ask can Ireland ever be saved?

The MPs all speak of peace,
But all they want is that piece
Of land, home to them all,
How many more like rain must fall?

So this is the end, the end of what?
Of what could be, but what is not,
Because British betrayal in 1916,
Means peace in Ireland will never be seen.

Chris Brady (16)
St Leonard's RC Comprehensive School

SPIRIT OF LIFE

Look through your eyes,
Open them and see.
What lies ahead of you?
An eternity of trying to do your best.

Listen to your heart,
What is it saying?
Follow the steps
That have been set out before you.

Open your mind and look closely,
At what the future may hold.
Sink into time,
Let nothing stop you.

The future is for hope,
But the present is for action.
Life is for living,
But the spirit is for eternity.

Sarah Wigham (16)
St Leonard's RC Comprehensive School

LIFE

When we're with different people,
We're still on our own.
We're all made out of
Different stone.

We all look alike, dress alike,
And act alike.
But our thoughts and feelings,
Come from our soul.

But if you understood me,
And I understood you,
And we all got along,
There'd be nothing to do.

Would the world lack meaning,
Psychology too,
If you understood me,
And I understood you?

Nicola Goodburn (16)
St Leonard's RC Comprehensive School

CHANGE NOW!

People can be nasty, people can be nice
Some people eat chips, some people eat rice
Some people are black, some people are white
Some people are peaceful, some people will fight
Some people end up locked in a cell
Others will burn forever in hell
But people in general are all the same
We are all house-trained and usually tame
We sometimes laugh, we sometimes cry
One day we will all die
We all have a mam, we all have a dad
We may turn out good, we may turn out bad
We all need to eat, and we all need to sleep
We all have memories we want to keep
We all have an important part to play
In the making of each and every day
It is up to some of us to go and teach
Others to travel the world and preach
We are doomed according to our prophetic men
For war will strike us all again
But what could we fight over today
Conditions, creed, race or pay?
I hope we will not have to fight again
As it would certainly end the rule of men
Our planet would be completely destroyed
Our right to rule it, null and void
But we all have hope, we must not despair
Luckily today most people do care,
So I believe we will all be good
And we will never again shed innocent blood.

Mark Fleming (16)
St Leonard's RC Comprehensive School

ANTICIPATION

My mind ticks over,
I stand and I watch,
Can I actually do it?
The fear and excitement,.
The rush through your body,
But,
Dare I actually do it?
The crowd is growing,
The anticipation's there,
Shall I actually do it?
My friends think 'yes'!
A few think 'no'!
I've decided I'm going to do it.
Most think it's great,
Some think it's silly,
Am I daft to do it?
Tied in, is it safe?
My body starts to shake,
My hands go numb,
My legs are weak,
It looks like I'm going to do it.
In I go.
Slowly, slowly up it rises,
The solid iron cage,
The tension rises, breath is held,
Must I actually do it?
I'm at the top
My mind is racing
I am going to do it!
The heart is thumping,
But, isn't that what it's all about?
The art of bungee jumping.

Jade Mackie (16)
St Leonard's RC Comprehensive School

CONSCIENCE

There she stood all stiff and rigid
Not a muscular movement in sight
For he was present in the room
So there she stood in fright.

It wasn't his manner
Nor his face
That scared this poor girl stiff
It was his longing, lasting, lingering yet frightening, scary gaze.

Everywhere there he was
Everywhere she went
She could not rid this desperate man,
She knew she'd have to repent.

It wasn't like it was her fault
He forced her to be there
To commit that sinful crime
Did he really care?

Ever since that memorable day,
He followed here and there
She knew he'd catch her sometime near
The waiting she'd have to bear.

A man had died in that crime
Was she really to blame?
Why had he made her do it?
A life lost by her shame.

She could not help the way she felt
It was as if she was possessed
She knew it was not her fault
For it was him that was obsessed.

For on this day the lady knew
What she had to do
To confront this man there and then
But who was he? Who?

Emma Ward (16)
St Leonard's RC Comprehensive School

Up The Wall

The rope is holding well, out there in the crag.
The wind blowing in my face, as I dive into my chalk bag.

I insert another karabiner, into the rock so sharp
The feeling of the dangerous wild, the dawning of the dark.

Pat is on the ground, holding the dead man so stiff.
As I retrieve my hammer from my harness, hanging off the cliff.

With my Boreal boots and harness, I clamber to the top.
A real sense of achievement is gained, I wish it would never stop.

Into the depths of the Cobbler, The Highlands most proud and distinct.
I have come to tackle its faces, and hopefully again I think.

The bleak and desolate mountain, is an attraction which gives a
                challenge,
Scaling the great Loch Long, surrounded by Ime and Narin

Many climbers pay respect to the mountain which gives no mercy.
My visit proved me lucky, not all can leave so easily.

Kieran Brookes (13)
St Leonard's RC Comprehensive School

Cycle

Retniw
Cold sun. Grey days.
Tornadoes tickling teeth.
Detached finger protectors, dawning
Dark before
Bedtime.

Gnirps
Luminous buds. Fresh breaths.
Pregnancies end.
Uncertain newness.
Trickling life source
Flowing freely
On.
Stretch. Scratch. Awaken. After
Bedtime.

Remmus
Hot winds. Yellow nights.
Red sun licking lawns.
Sugared breezes through
Open windows.
Children - mature
Play after
Bedtime.

Nmutua
Lives end. Lives fall.
End.
Terminal.
Await.
Darkness.
Meet.
Bedtime.

Sarah-Jane Mason (17)
St Leonard's RC Comprehensive School

THE SPIRIT OF THE SON

The Earth shook under the murky gloom
As the mutilated man rose out of his tomb

His one-fingered hand gripped the muddy floor
As the frightened figure rose back up once more.

The blood-spattered creature from where he lay
Set off from his tomb to live another day!

His one battered eye scanned the graveyard dark
His body, unrecognisable cold and stark.

He prowled the street, seeking his house
The night air was cold, quiet as a mouse.

He stepped unsteadily, scared of people around
Its arm almost severed as blood dripped to the ground.

At last the figure reached the house and knocked on the door
Where he waited to see his family once more.

Andrew Murray (13)
St Leonard's RC Comprehensive School

BROTHERS

B rothers think they know everything
R ant and rave to go and play
O ften go to play football
T heir music is terrible, they play it full blast
H og the TV every day
E xcellent at being sarcastic
R ude to me
S ometimes nice!

Vicki Howard (12)
St Leonard's RC Comprehensive School

COTTAGE ON THE HILL

Far away from anything else,
Situated high on a hill,
Stands the cottage of an old couple,
Surrounded by quietness and dark.

Rocking in their chairs sit the old couple,
Close to the fire, as if protecting them,
When heard is a loud knock at the door,
The couple both jump with fear.

The old man rises from his chair,
He goes to the door and opens it,
His wife observes carefully with watchful eyes,
He carefully opens the door.

As he looks out, he sees no one through the dark,
But the scent of his recently dead son,
Lingers in the air around the door,
And a piece of clothing lies by the step.

His wife accompanies him at the door,
And sees the evidence of her son,
She screams with delight and calls his name,
As her husband stands back and locks the door.

The scared old man prays for this to end,
A sudden flash of lightning,
Is seen outside, accompanied by a loud bang,
And finally all evidence of their son disappears.

Charlotte Kerr (13)
St Leonard's RC Comprehensive School

Long Lost

Seek and search believe in lies
Forever you'll see you'll die,
But hunt, kill, stab, shoot and burn
Follow instinct you will learn,
Back to your roots
Of man's dispute,
Back to your roots
You can't pollute,
BC before the chaos
Little babe Jesus take us,
Cry for God if he does hear
Let him know I hate it here.
Back to your roots
Past Eden's fruit,
Back to the roots
Take Satan's loot.
Modern legal things to do
In the list not me or you.
Hassling from the techno-world
I liked the fear from which I'm hurled
Bent, twisted beyond belief
Screaming out to get relief
Yesterday came from the soul
Now you're empty pay the toll.
Back to your roots
My ancient roots.
Back to the roots.
Ancestral roots.
Back to your roots
Spiritual roots.
Back to the roots
The sacred roots.

Geoffrey Burgess (13)
St Leonard's RC Comprehensive School

WHAT'S BEHIND ME?

Through the darkness,
I hurried along,
A bang, a crash,
Was that a bomb?

My spine was tingling,
With visions of fear,
Shivers poured down my spine,
It made me tremble and shed a tear.

My legs like jelly and
Hands like ice,
Whatever is behind me
Definitely isn't mice.

Hurry, hurry I said to myself,
There's something after me,
I tripped and cut open my knee,
But whatever it was, it was after *me!*

Shelley Griffin (13)
St Leonard's RC Comprehensive School

STEAM IS LIKE . . .

Steam is powder,
Steam is white,
Steam is power,
Steam is hot,
Steam is cloud,
Steam is cotton,
Steam is snow.

It's made from water,
It comes out of the kettle,
It comes from the train,
And makes it go,
It makes good shapes,
It's interesting to watch,
Look up at the clouds,
It's amazing to see.

Adam Nicholson (13)
St Leonard's RC Comprehensive School

TEACHER FROM HEAVEN

A teacher from heaven
Tries hard to understand
Everyone in class, me even
Allows for mistakes
Caring, for he knows
How hard I try
Every day to
Right, whoops, write and multiply.

For some it's
Really difficult
Others it's not
Making sense of, such a lot.

However he gets
Everyone's attention and affection
As he's so fair and caring
Very friendly and kind
Endeavouring to enrich my
Not so bright mind.

Peter Hewitt (13)
St Leonard's RC Comprehensive School

THE DARK, SCARY NIGHT

As the night groaned out
At the passers-by,
And the lightning shook
Above from the sky.

The rain poured down,
Getting worse and worse,
Soaking the town,
But the passers-by went on.

The thunder roared
And shook the night.
The passers-by
Screamed out in fright.

As they heard shouts,
From a nearby street,
They saw some people
They didn't want to meet.

Rowdy, loud and drunk,
It appeared
'They might come closer',
The couple feared.

A car came past,
And lit up the street.
The passers-by wished
They could rest their feet.

As they turned the corner,
They heard a shout.
Oh, how they wished
They hadn't gone out.

So the couple went home
And rested their feet,
And warmed themselves
In the homely heat.

The couple sat down
Glad to be away
And waiting anxiously
For the next day.

Cora Hanson (14)
St Leonard's RC Comprehensive School

CRUNCHING BONES

The lively, young son drives off to work,
Deep in the shadows, the grasps of death lurk,
Lovingly waves 'bye to his father and mother,
Never again they all will discover.
Hear the bones go crunch, crunch, crunch.

As he locks the car door, he suspects nothing,
Soon nothing to look at but the wood of a coffin,
Shivering, he jogs across the car park,
Soon, there's only dark, dark, dark.
Hear the bones go crunch, crunch, crunch.

The cogs and the wheels go round and round,
Metal against metal, makes a grinding sound,
The screeching sound echoes around the room,
The victim whistles, oblivious to the oncoming doom.
Hear the bones go crunch, crunch, crunch.

The goggle eyes, hear the poor lad scream,
Muscles and limbs ripped at the seams,
Mouths agape, the whirring ends,
With such a loss, only time will mend.
Hear the bones go crunch, crunch, crunch.

Emma Kitching (13)
St Leonard's RC Comprehensive School

DUNBLANE

This mad man came with guns, so bright,
He ended sixteen young children's lives.
He wandered into the school gym,
Oh why, oh why did he choose them?

Their parents stood waiting anxiously,
To see if their family had been hit by tragedy.
Relief came for many waiting there,
But sixteen parents had lost their bairns.

Guns should've been banned long ago,
Then of this tragedy we'd never know.
A song was sung as a sign of respect,
To remember the children we'll never forget.

This mad man came with guns so bright,
He ended sixteen young children's lives.
The whole world mourned for what he'd done,
Why, oh why, did he use a gun?

Laura Smith (13)
St Leonard's RC Comprehensive School

OH, SO JEALOUS NIGHT

So jealous night,
You take the stars which once gleamed in his eyes
His sweet smell you steal to create your astonishing perfume
You have drawn the dark mystery out of him which I so desired
Oh so jealous night
You have slain my love
And now I am yours.

Sarah Villis (17)
St Leonard's RC Comprehensive School

THE CURSE
(Inspired by 'The Monkey's Paw')

The night was cold and very wet
The ground was just a mess
Inside, the father and his son
Were sitting playing chess.

A knock upon the door was heard
Which gave them both a fright
Then Sergeant Major Morris came
Towards them from the night.

He told a tale of strange events
In lands across the sea
Where plagues and deeds and wars occurred
How frightening they could be.

Then from the pocket of his coat
He drew a monkey's paw
He held it high for all to see
Then told a tale of awe.

A spell had been put upon this paw
To give each man three wishes
He waved the paw with trembling hands
Above the dinner dishes.

'Twice have I wished' he said out loud
'A third I don't desire
This paw's bad luck' he said, with fear
And threw it on the fire.

'The reason why I burnt the paw'
He said with bated breath
'A third wish made by any man
Would soon bring certain death.'

Andrea Muers (13)
St Leonard's RC Comprehensive School

LEAVING

I hated leaving my hometown,
My friends, school and street,
I moved to a new place,
Where there were new people to meet.

They all have different accents,
Which I can hardly understand,
Because mine is totally different,
Like as if I'm from a different land.

I have fitted in quite well here,
But there are friends I do quite miss,
I like to phone them every night,
And have a chat and a gossip.

I miss my old house in the city,
It's so different to the country,
Big shops and a busy town,
To little shops and fields aplenty.

But now I like it quite a lot,
I've got lots of friends and I'm happy,
I'd hate to move again somewhere
Because the people here are nice and chatty!

Helen Timothy (14)
St Leonard's RC Comprehensive School

SHADOWS

It creeps about across the cold floor,
It follows you as you walk out the door,
No matter where you are day or night,
That thing's face will never enter light.

It lurks in the darkness up the high walls,
It hides in the leaves in the middle of Fall,
You call out for it to come to your face,
But no matter where you are, in whatever place,
It won't come.

Verity Williams (14)
St Leonard's RC Comprehensive School

THE FIGURE

The house looms eerily in the dark,
Old shutters swing on creaky hinges,
Floorboards creak as the house groans,
The figure approaches with a grinding of bones.

The old woman hears it, her breath in rasps,
Eyes as wide as wheels, her mouth agape,
Sits defensively with knuckles of white,
What fate awaits on this woe-begotten night?

The door opens and shuts with a slam,
The figure has entered; she freezes rigid,
Shadows pass along the wall,
Silently pacing down the hall.

The figure hisses as it draws near the room,
It arches its back and bares its teeth.
Its eyes pierce everything in sight,
It targets the room ready for a fight.

It's in the room upon her now,
It stares at her a hungry glare.
She breathes out relief as it jumps on her knee,
For it is Felix the cat, come back for his tea!

Catriona Long (13)
St Leonard's RC Comprehensive School

A Loving Mother's Sorrow

If only they had heeded the Sergeant Major's warning
Her son would be alive as each new day was dawning.
If only he had not retrieved that wretched monkey's paw
But left it in the blazing fire her heart would not be sore.

Her son had suggested money; he couldn't have been more wrong,
For when their wish was granted, their son's life didn't last long.
Was the price of his existence worth a mere two hundred pounds?
His mother would give up all she had to hear him make a sound.

Gazing out of the window, seeing nothing at all,
The mother sits and waits for her lost son to call.
She wants him back so badly, she can't believe he's gone,
She loved him but she lost him, how can her life go on?

Helen Sharp (13)
St Leonard's RC Comprehensive School

England

We're in France for '98,
Even though we left it late.
We thought we would not qualify,
We thought this Cup would pass us by.
England were strong in every game,
To give us fans our ultimate aim.
Our only defeat came at Wembley,
Came off those men from Italy.
But we paid them back well in Rome,
Snatching a point at their home.
We'll go to France with the world's best teams,
And show them up. England will make our dreams.

Andrew Steel (14)
St Leonard's RC Comprehensive School

A Curse

The curse of a cruel man hangs over your head,
If you don't watch out you may end up dead.

The curse which lies on the charm,
Was put there to cause harm.
The man who did place it upon this,
Wants you to make just one wish.

The curse of a cruel man hangs over your head,
If you don't watch out you may end up dead.

The wish that you will want to make,
Will really not much time take.
The eerie feeling that it gives,
Shows you that the curse still lives.

The curse of a cruel man hangs over your head,
If you don't act wisely you may end up dead.

Wish to be rich and happy,
And you will be a sad chappy.
The way it's granted will make you amazed,
It will really leave you very changed.

The curse of a cruel man hangs over your head,
If you don't act wisely you may end up dead.

When the wish is used up and gone,
It is all said and done.
The pain that it once caused you,
Will now happen to someone else too.

Emily Dott (13)
St Leonard's RC Comprehensive School

DEATH

The machines that took my life last week
Continue to work as normal.
The men morosely carry on,
Trying to hide their mourning.

Workmen whistle - they try to lift
The damp, sad air that hangs
Over the factory, through the town,
Throughout the local land.

My unseen figure slowly follows
The noisy horse-drawn cart.
The funeral procession walks steadily on,
My Mother and Father distraught.

I see her tear-stained face approach
The coffin where I lie.
I know she feels my presence near,
But she doesn't quite know why.

She does not understand the reason
That my short life must end.
The comforting words from friends she hears
Do nothing to ease the pain.

My Father talks quietly to the priest.
Does he know that only his greed
That caused my pain and suffering,
His selfish grasping deed?

Our closest friends and family,
Follow us to the house.
My Father offers a supporting arm
To his distressed and tearful spouse.

So now I leave them on their own
Our friends and family gone.
I say my final au revoir
But my spirit still lives on.

Aileen Dennis (13)
St Leonard's RC Comprehensive School

WHISPERS ON THE WIND

With pain in her heart, and guilt in her head,
The old woman makes her way up to bed,
And as she breaks down on the stairs with a cry,
The moon looks on and the wind whispers by.

They'd made their wish and ignored the warning,
So now, the sun doesn't shine in the morning.
It's blocked by the clouds, so dull in the sky,
Tossed like waves as the wind whispers by.

Their ill-gotten gains, had brought them such sorrow,
They'd lost something they couldn't buy, steal or borrow.
Their only son was the price of their sins,
Now the fakir's laughter drifts by on the wind.

The sadness she feels digs a hole in her heart,
After all of these years it still tears her apart.
So now she's alone, and longing to die,
But afraid of hell's fire with no wind whispering by.

Helen Burnip (13)
St Leonard's RC Comprehensive School

WORDS

Some say words aren't enough,
But I say they're wrong.
Words can build you up,
Words can bring you down.
When the tears are falling
And you can't see the light,
A word from a friend
Can give you new sight.
But with the lashing of the tongue,
That devil's spear will have its fun,
'Cos sticks and stones
Can break your bones
But calling hurts much more.
Say it in your head, word, word, word,
Such a small word.
But big things come in small packages,
I would like a word
A word of warning
Let me know if you get word
I'll give you my word
Because you only have to say the word
And I say this by word of mouth.
In short a word is,
What you should take me at,
So learn your words,
They are enough
To teach, to guide, to seek, to find,
To use your mind,
So whether a poet or writer
If you use the smallest single meaningful speech.
One thing to remember,
Word perfection is something
You can reach.

Joanne Walls (13)
St Leonard's RC Comprehensive School

DEAD MAN WAKING!

The night was dark,
The wind was still,
The corpse arose,
'Twas his night to kill.

His body was torn,
His face was white,
His limbs were hanging
On this ill-begotten night.

He made his way
Without a sound,
To the dreary house
That he was bound.

He opened the window
Climbed into the room,
He looked at the woman
Soon to be doomed.

And with a great cry,
He drew out a knife,
Ran over to the lady,
Who'd be robbed of her life.

He plunged the knife
Into her chest,
She would never now
Waken from her rest.

And as the sun began to rise,
Into a new, twinkling day,
He ran back to the graveyard
Where he would forever lay.

Natasha Van Leempoel (13)
St Leonard's RC Comprehensive School

HERBERT'S DEATH

That scream stopped everyone dead.
It was a high-pitched scream.
A scream of terror,
A scream of pain.

It brought everyone to Herbert White's machinery,
Whatever they had been doing was forgotten.
Their eyes widened,
And their jaws dropped.

His scream echoed through the factory again,
He had caught his hand
Jammed between revolving metal wheels,
Metal that was slowly crushing him.

The dull cogs compressed his hand,
Crunched it up.
In the silence people heard the sharp snap of bones,
And saw the blood gush out.

The blood stained the machinery,
It smeared on Herbert's mangled flesh.
It shone bright red under the factory's yellow lights,
And still more poured out.

His arm became lodged in the machinery,
His lower arm ripped and tore,
His elbow bone split and shattered,
His upper arm twisted and cut.

Herbert's screaming now descended to a loud sob,
His lungs exhausted from his last effort.
People now started to recover their wits,
They shouted for the equipment to be shut off.

But it was too late!
The machine crawled toward Herbert's neck and head.
He struggled in vain to get away,
He shrieked from the bottom his chest.

But it was all useless,
The final scream was hideously cut short,
And people hid their eyes,
As Herbert White's skull was crushed.

Stephen Grace (14)
St Leonard's RC Comprehensive School

THE MAGICAL MONKEY'S PAW

Slowly and stiffly he moves his limbs
As he rises from the floor.
Woken from the dead
By a mummified monkey's paw.

Called to go to his parents' house,
He walks barefooted on the grassy turf,
Beyond the still, silent graveyard,
He knows he should not be on this earth.

But the paw keeps on calling,
And the house comes into sight.
He bangs loudly on the front door
But there is no response, just the silence of the night.

He knocks again and the chain rattles,
But there is no longer a call from the monkey's paw.
The door opens but nobody is there,
Because now he rests where he was before.

Philip Magowan (13)
St Leonard's RC Comprehensive School

CAR

Faster than anything from Mother Nature,
Growling, purring at the touch of a pedal.
Beautifully crafted, every curve, every feature,
The glint of the sun on the gleaming metal.

Effortlessly efficient in its mechanical splendour,
Slicing its way through tortoise-like drivers.
Screaming ahead is the chrome-plated fender,
But the showroom image disguises another side.

The bumper, now stained with blood and fumes,
Knocks down millions, chokes many more.
No one stops to think, they simply assume,
That they're doing no harm in their smart four by four.

Gavin Bainbridge (17)
St Leonard's RC Comprehensive School

THE WALKING DEAD!

An anguished cry is heard,
As a disembodied soul drags himself from
His eternal resting place.
His eyes expressionless, face vacant,
His shambling walk is clumsy and lethargic,
The hideous corpse is drawn to its final destiny,
A loud knock shudders through the house,
As the old man frantically searches for the monkey's paw,
The gruesome corpse stands motionless with his fingers
Clutched to the knocker,
The door opens and a cold wind sweeps up the stairs,
So the mutilated corpse returns to its eternal resting place.

Kenneth Fox (13)
St Leonard's RC Comprehensive School

THE NIGHT OF THE LIVING DEAD

The grave-keeper departs, the yard is left empty,
The under-soil ferociously begins to shake,
The mysterious songs of the night-time begin,
Which owls and bats curiously make.

The sun has disappeared behind the earth,
The darkness inspires the dead,
And from the empty silence of a grave,
There suddenly appears a head.

All around the deserted graveyard,
Corpses are coming to life.
The father, the mother, the sister and brother
Even the husband and wife.

Midnight comes and the party begins,
The deathly music is rising high,
It seems just like your very nightmare,
Until disturbed by the cockerel's cry.

Like bullets flying from a gun,
The corpses return to their beds.
The sun appears, and brightens the place,
As the dead pull their tombstones over their heads.

The day begins, the streets are busy,
And you know what is to be said,
When the sun disappears, behind the earth
It becomes the night of the living dead.

Catie Durbridge (13)
St Leonard's RC Comprehensive School

THE MYSTERIOUS HOUSE

The lonely house just stands there still,
With an ancient couple upon a hill.
The windows creak and then you shake
In the deathly silence waiting for one to break.

The sound of the sly trees slowly swishing on the windows,
While the enormous garden stands at the back
                           with just the scent of a red rose.
The floorboards creak and scare you to death,
As one of them breaks you think you could
                           have taken your last breath.

The house stands frightening and tall,
With cobwebs, dust and creepy spiders up the wall.
It looks over the whole village at night,
With really curious, noisy people in sight.

The dusky, dark, demeaning atmosphere of this dirty place,
Sends shivers up and down the spine and even tears down the face,
As people wave past, terrified to step in.
It's so lonely and quiet you can hear anything, even a pin!

The sound of the sly trees slowly swishing on the windows,
While the enormous garden stands at the back
                           with just the scent of a rose.
The floorboards creak and scare you to death,
As one of them breaks you think you could
                           have taken your *last breath*.

Kate Hopgood (13)
St Leonard's RC Comprehensive School

DON'T MEDDLE WITH MAGIC
(Inspired by 'The Monkey's Paw')

Outside the cosy house,
The wind can be heard to roar.
The comfortable inside await,
A knock upon their door.

The visitor stands awaiting,
And then is drawn inside.
Contentedly he sips his whisky,
At the fireside.

Telling enthralling travelling tales,
And rumours of a monkey's paw,
The family absorbed and entertained,
Ever wanting more.

The evil fairy-tale stories,
Become a little scary.
The mother and father huddle
As they become more wary.

From warnings to wonderful wishes
The father thinks ahead.
He picks up the putrid paw,
No more warnings are said.

The first wish is quickly granted,
In a very subtle way.
The young son's life, for money
Is such a dear price to pay.

Rebecca Armstrong (13)
St Leonard's RC Comprehensive School

TRAPPED FOREVER

As the ancient church clock struck twelve at night,
The town was bare, nothing living in sight.
On the last chime the ground did shake,
The ground trembled, as they began to wake.

Dead and buried six feet under,
The sky was black, with a roar of thunder.
The ground erupted, emerged the deceased,
Trapped souls on this earth for tonight at least.

Decaying flesh, disfigured limbs, disgusting smell,
Trapped on this earth, no heaven, no hell.
In the small town, the victims await,
Peacefully sleeping, not knowing their fate.

The corpse stumbles towards the front door,
About to get revenge, about to break the law.
It's all their fault, they're all to blame,
My death was no accident, 'life's just a game'.

'My revenge I must get to put the past behind,
They deserve it, they shouldn't mind.'
He enters the home of his childhood,
Before he was buried and covered with mud.

Looking down on his victims, about to kill,
His mind races, freedom in sight, until!
The ancient church clock struck one,
His only chance had gone.

Shrieking with despair, shrivelling to the floor,
They would have been dead with one minute more.
A heap of stinking flesh, lying there, all limp and lame,
Then all of a sudden he burst into flame.

Trapped on this earth, for all eternity,
His last and only opportunity.
So say your prayers it could be you,
To go to heaven you have to join a queue.

Or you could be stuck like many more,
Read this tale, it's not to ignore.
So when you are deceased,
May you *Rest In Peace!*

Amy Corrigan (13)
St Leonard's RC Comprehensive School

IRONY

Over the top,
the excitement, the exhilaration, the fear.
Trudging through the mud,
he falls heavy, like lead,
his clothes sodden with dark, thick blood.
He feels the pain - piercing, sharp,
the pull towards the next life, drags him to unconsciousness.

He wakes to the silence of all but his breath,
choking, spluttering,
death draws near.
He's alone, afraid.
In the darkness of his thoughts, he drifts towards the night.
The distant sounds of triumphant bells
toll for him in his final throes.
He leaves, and yet behind him stays
the joyous sounds of victory.

Elizabeth Finn (18)
St Leonard's RC Comprehensive School

A Curse On A Monkey's Paw

In the deepest depths of the Amazon jungle
A witch doctor started to curse
A monkey's paw, full of evil,
To teach three men a lesson or worse.

He chanted the spell to his gods,
Concentrating for it mustn't be wrong.
The gods must give it their magic,
As the witch doctor bellowed his song.

The paw would create sorrow,
The paw would reflect on one's sin.
If your wish should concern greed
It would make your life so grim.

So the monkey's paw was born,
It went all to the witch doctor's plans,
For it would cause disaster
If it fell into the wrong hands.

Jonathan Kitching (13)
St Leonard's RC Comprehensive School

Paindrops

The droplet ran down the moist glass,
Like tears cooling the hot cheeks.
She sat there and wept -
Hoping that the pain would be washed away
Leaving a rainbow scar.
And, so the grey subsided and blue
Blotted the cloud-filled sky -
The droplet ceased to exist and a smile crept
Over the stained face.

Jill Mulcahy (17)
St Leonard's RC Comprehensive School

WHERE ARE YOU NOW?

I've never lost anyone
close to me before that time
I don't think I really
understood death until then.
I didn't realise the pain
or the tears that I would shed.

I miss you still now, and
I want to see you, now.
I can't believe what happened
or why.
I think of you a lot when
I'm alone at night in bed.

Where are you now?
I really want to see you.
Someone so alive like you were,
can't cease to be.
You must be out there somewhere,
but where?

Please, please will you let me know
in some way, that you're ok?
I really miss you and
I really want to see you.
But where are you now?
Are you still there?

Grace Potter (15)
St Leonard's RC Comprehensive School

GAZE

I look into your eyes,
Searching for the key,
And it comes to my surprise
When I find you staring at me.

I see you blink,
I feel you there,
And as I think
I lose my stare.

I remember the day
I looked at heaven above,
I remember the day
I fell in love.

Emma Hutton (17)
St Leonard's RC Comprehensive School

TEACHER...

F orever helping others
R eading so perfect
O riginal beauty
M otivating children

H aving fun
E verlasting education
A ttractive voice
V ery caring
E asy to talk to
N ever uninteresting.

Peter Rodriguez (13)
St Leonard's RC Comprehensive School

ROMEO & JULIET

Star-crossed lovers whose paths would end,
In their families making amends.
The story begins at the ball of the Capulets,
When Romeo first saw Juliet.
But Romeo and Juliet knew their love could never be,
And later their death would be their destiny.

Romeo and Juliet married secretly
But still their families kept fighting repeatedly.
Fights continued and deaths of Mercutio and Tybalt,
Which the prince said was Romeo's fault,
And so Romeo had to leave Verona city
While Juliet wallowed in her own self-pity.
Married to an exile who she would never see,
This wasn't the way she'd planned their lives to be.

Never to see Romeo, there was only one notion,
To go to Friar Lawrence and find a sleeping potion.
That night before sleep she drank the potion down,
Dead her parents thought when she was found.
Romeo came to see his love - Juliet,
And in a shocked fret
He killed himself with poison just as Juliet woke,
No words did either speak
And with Romeo's dagger Juliet ended her life
As Romeo's loving wife.

Nicola Siberry (17)
St Leonard's RC Comprehensive School

WHO?

They said she was beautiful,
She was adored.
Wherever she went,
People talked.
She walked into a room,
Everybody stopped.
That stunning figure,
Those majestic eyes,
Who?

Two drivers, one dark night,
It all ended
Her face destroyed,
Everything gone.
She was nothing,
Face, body or soul.
Who?

Still alive today,
Alone and dejected.
Who cares?
Forgotten forever,
Faded away.
'She' is all I was.
Who?

Laura Edwards (17)
St Leonard's RC Comprehensive School

TEACHER FROM HEAVEN

My teacher from heaven would *never*,
Keep us behind the bell,
She'd let us out every night,
Right on the dong of the bell.

The amount of homework would be small,
That's if there was any at all!
We'd all love to have her,
That would be great,
'Cause she's the best of them all.

My teacher from heaven would *never*,
Keep us behind the bell,
She'd let us out every night,
Right on the dong of the bell.

Mark Henderson (13)
St Leonard's RC Comprehensive School

THE WALK

One dark night as I
walked through the wood
an owl hooted as a
signal to all creatures
that an intruder was present.

The crack of a twig and
the dampness underfoot
awoke me
I found myself alone and
isolated in the dark.
I cry out and I am answered
by *silence*.

Christopher Veitch (17)
St Leonard's RC Comprehensive School

THE TEACHER FROM HEAVEN

What's a teacher from heaven?
A fair person.
What's a teacher from heaven?
A no homework mad-man.
What's a teacher from heaven?
A no detention mad-man.
What's a teacher from heaven?
A helpful person.
What's a teacher from heaven?
A patient person.
What's a teacher from heaven?
A fun, talkative person.
What's a teacher from heaven?
An attractive, caring person.
What's a teacher from heaven?
A person who joins in conversations.
That's the teacher from heaven.

Emma Liddle (13)
St Leonard's RC Comprehensive School

TEACHER!

F iery breath
R isen from death
O bligation to be bad
M akes his pupils sad.

H orrible frown
E ven wears the devil's crown
L iving to give detention
L aughing as he shouts attention.

Robert Garside (13)
St Leonard's RC Comprehensive School

TEACHER FROM HELL!

There was a teacher from hell,
That didn't ring the bell,
He smoked,
I wished he'd choke,
There was a teacher from hell.

He's smelly,
He's called Kelly,
We fought,
And he put people on report,
He was the teacher from hell.

Daryl Hodgson (13)
St Leonard's RC Comprehensive School

TEACHER FROM HELL

Horribly I was told to leave the room
Horribly he said 'You're on detention'
Horribly he told me to finish my work
Horribly he shouted 'Homework is hard'
Horribly I thought this teacher was from hell.

Daniel Bell (13)
St Leonard's RC Comprehensive School

Teacher From...

H appy
E ver ready to help
A bsolutely marvellous
V ery pleasant to talk to
E ven likes to play football
N ever gives you homework!

James Lonergan (13)
St Leonard's RC Comprehensive School

A Rainy Day

Rain is boring
especially on Sunday
it stops me from going out
when I hear a splash
it makes my heart crash.
Rain is boring
especially on Sunday.

>Rain is scary
>especially if it is all night
>it sometimes gives me a fright
>I wish it wouldn't rain
>oh I wish it wouldn't.
>Rain is scary
>especially if it is all night.

Sharon Price (11)
Shotton Hall Comprehensive School

The Summer's Gone

As I look out my window,
Across the fields so far,
I dream of long summer nights,
Which are slowly passing me by.

> The darker nights are drawing near,
> As behind my curtains I sit,
> Wishing for the winter months,
> To rush by me so quick.

The streets are paved with darkness,
I wish they were paved with gold,
The brilliance of sunshine,
Is such a sight to behold.

Danielle Coils (11)
Shotton Hall Comprehensive School

Dark

In the dark you can't see a thing,
You hear noises in the street,
Wondering what they are,
Are they there to scare you?
Dustbins falling over,
Cars in the street,
Sometimes their horns beep,
Noises in the street
Sometimes scare me.

Do they scare you?

Cherrelle Docherty (11)
Shotton Hall Comprehensive School

Seasons

Spring
Sun is setting high in the sky
Flowers blooming from the ground
Lambs leaping up and down
Birds are busy building nests
This is the season of no rest.

Summer
Sun is blazing in the air
People having fun everywhere
Bees are buzzing they're such a pest
But still this is the season I love best.

Autumn
Leaves are lying on the ground
Hedgehogs crawling round and round
The wind is dwelling up above
This is the season that I love.

Winter
Snow is falling swiftly down
Lying gracefully on the ground
Children playing, having fun
This is the season with no sun.

Gill McGowan (12)
Shotton Hall Comprehensive School

FOOTBALL FANTASY

Football is my passion
My life, my aim, my goal
It will keep me out of prison
And also off the dole.

To see me play at Wembley
Would make my mother cry,
And if I lift a trophy high
Then surely she would die.

To see me play at Wembley
Would be a dream come true
To hear the people shout and cheer
Would fill my heart with glee,
And make me cry with pride and joy
If it's with the Toon army.

Kevin Swann (11)
Shotton Hall Comprehensive School

THE WILD ONE

The big black horse so strong and bold,
It's beautiful but never rode,
It rears and bucks out in the field,
With all that might I'd hate to be near,
But it carries on out there strong,
Making it seem like the scary one,
It acts so hard and tries to be mean,
But after all it is the Wild One.

Michelle Lacey (12)
Shotton Hall Comprehensive School

SCHOOL

As I walk into the school yard
I see new faces,
New teachers,
New uniforms,
New coats.
I feel happy.

But when I walk into the school
I see the same dull walls,
Same old chairs,
Same old desk,
Same old drawers.
I feel sad.
But then comes in happy laughing children
I feel happy again
As they sit down to listen to me.

Samantha Hutchinson (11)
Shotton Hall Comprehensive School

MY FIRST DAY AT SHOTTON HALL

My first day at school,
Was really cool,
I was really nervous at first,

I thought I would get lost,
But of course I did not,
Only because there were people to show me around.

It was home time at last,
The day went very fast,
There was nothing to be nervous about at all.

Deonne Heatlie (11)
Shotton Hall Comprehensive School

MY FRIEND FRED

Spiders are clever, spiders are great,
You should see the cobwebs upon our gate,
Some of them round, and some of then square,
When you walk past they get in your hair.

Some of them large, and some of them small,
They stretch from the gate to the top of the wall,
He climbs so high
I hope he won't fall.

They look so silky and shimmery at night,
When I go with my torch and shine a light,
I can see a little fly all wrapped in a cocoon,
Waiting for a spider, he will be coming soon.

My spider looks friendly,
I nick-named him Fred
Perhaps he won't eat it,
And go to bed instead.

First thing this morning I thought he was lost,
When I saw his web all covered in frost,
Up came the sunshine to warm up his bed,
Guess who crawled out?
My friend Fred.

Jennifer Collins (11)
Shotton Hall Comprehensive School

HALLOWE'EN

The sky is blue,
the grass is green
but nothing's so scary
as Hallowe'en.
That knock on the door
who could it be?
A goblin or witch
or even a ghost.
That chill on that night
gives you a fright.
Some say it is
a witches' party night
but some just say
Hallowe'en, Hallowe'en!
       Hallowe'en!

Christopher Mooney (11)
Shotton Hall Comprehensive School

AUTUMN

Leaves multicolour
Red, yellow, brown crispy as crisps
The grass is not green
It is yellow, also dead
Dead and dry, paths in ice
Ground frozen, morning nippy
Night ice-cold
The birds are not singing
The bees are not buzzing
The trees are bare
Leaves on the ground.

Paul Docherty (11)
Shotton Hall Comprehensive School

THE MOON, THE EARTH AND THE SUN

The sun is too hot,
Too hot to handle.
The moon is cold,
It'll give you frostbite.
The earth is warm,
Not too hot and not too cold,
Just right for mankind to handle.

        If you lived on the sun,
        You'd fry
        If you lived on the moon
        You'd die.
        If you lived on the earth
        You'd live.

So live on the earth,
Not the sun,
And not the moon.

Amanda Rain (12)
Shotton Hall Comprehensive School

SEA

The sea is like a big blue blanket
Crashing against a pillow of rocks
There's brown fish, black fish swimming around
In it there's tropical fish too.
The sea is a vast place mile after nautical mile.
It is like a piece of blue silk waving in the wind.
Sail boats cruise across its surface.
Its water sparkles in the midday sun.
It's the deepest thing you've ever seen.

Jan Tinkler (11)
Shotton Hall Comprehensive School

MY FIRST DAY

How I remember my first day
I'd dreaded coming back
To school after the summer
I'd heard tales about older
Pupils flushing year sevens'
Heads down the toilet
I'd thought about if it
Ever happened to me
Time came for me to go
I was lost in a
World of people
I felt alone until I
Found all my friends
I didn't feel alone anymore.

Gareth Edwards (12)
Shotton Hall Comprehensive School

WHAT I SEE IN A RAINBOW

Seven colours make a rainbow
Red is danger and also hot
Yellow is springtime and when the birds sing
Pink is girlie and sugar and sweet
Green is grass for playing games
Purple is deep, deep as the ocean
Orange is sunny, juicy and sticky
Blue is for boys and the sky up above
That is how I see a rainbow.

Colin Flatt (11)
Shotton Hall Comprehensive School

THE SETTLING HOUSE

The house settles down,
the dog and cat are fed,
the children are bathed,
and tucked up in bed.

The parents lock up,
and retire for the night,
They walk up the stairs,
and turn out the light.

It's now around midnight,
there's no sound at all,
apart from the clock,
that ticks in the hall.

The night goes on,
the dawn reappears,
washing away the
night-time fears.

Deborah Watson (12)
Shotton Hall Comprehensive School

DEADLY SILENCE

As I look through the window
I see pain and despair,
But when I turn they are not there.
As I lie at night I hear noises crying, shouting
It gets louder and louder until bang!
Out of sight and sound,
And when it's all quiet no sound at all
It frightens so I call it
       Deadly silence.

Kayleigh Slater (11)
Shotton Hall Comprehensive School

THE COALMINE

It's very early I am out of bed
I need my breakfast I must be fed.

I go to the mine with pain and tears
Dying in the mine is the worst of my fears.

I puff and pant while I pull the truck
I reach a point where it gets stuck

It's afternoon my dinner's eaten
I don't go to sleep in case I'm beaten.

Some heavy coal falls on a man
People try to save him nobody can.

A man shouts 'Get out fast!'
People fall over as others push past.

A bang echoes as we jump to the ground
After five seconds there is no sound.

I got out safely at least this time,
Life is so dangerous down the mine.

David Iley (11)
Shotton Hall Comprehensive School

WINTER

Winter is here and so they say,
It's going to be a very cold day,
No birds in the trees,
No buzzing of bees,
As I look out of the window and watch the snow,
Sitting around my fire it's cosy you know.

The streets all covered in snow that's so white,
It stings my eyes as it's so crisp and bright.
The winter brings Santa, presents and toys,
There will be lots of happy girls and boys,
So as I release a very big sigh,
As I have watched another year go by.

Helen Haley (12)
Shotton Hall Comprehensive School

A DAY AT THE BEACH

The waves roared,
As the temperature soared
The day we went to the beach.
The children played
While the waves sprayed
The yellow sand in a heap.

The sand was hot,
In a sunny spot
The children jumped for joy.
All we heard was a great big splash
The wave had hit the boy.

The boy was wet,
As you can guess,
And so went for a swim.
You'll never guess what happened next
He lost his rubber ring.

The rubber ring went far away
The boy began to frown
The only thing that he could do
Was rush back into town.

Karl Gippert (11)
Shotton Hall Comprehensive School

NOVEMBER, NOVEMBER

November, November a time to remember!
Out in the street - with autumny blizzards.
Vines and trees, snow made by wizards!
Everlasting rain, everlasting winds.
My hat blows off in the cold autumn winds.
Bonfire Night - let's not forget the changing of clocks.
Early snow - All Souls Day - All Saints Day.
Remember the birds, not there anymore.
They have flown away where it is warmer,
                              and there is more food.
Day by day it rains - out there are some good things
                                        going on.
Autumn means Remembrance Day.
Poppies - soldiers - our country here.
Yes it's November.
Sad things, happy things, November, November.

Lauren Blower (11)
Shotton Hall Comprehensive School

SUN, MOON AND SPACE

Up there all around
In the darkness
Not a sound to be found
With the sun and its brightness
And the moon with its stars
Mercury, Venus, Earth and Mars
Not forgetting Jupiter and Saturn
With all those colours and beautiful patterns
All those stars and planets in the sky
Make people wonder why
Space is in the sky.

Victoria Kate Young (12)
Shotton Hall Comprehensive School

THE GHOST UP MY STREET

There's a ghost who lives just up my street,
He's actually quite a nice chap.
Every day he goes walking with his dog,
With a wooden stick and a bowler hat.

He's afraid of the dark.
Nothing like his Mam and Dad.
Always preferred the daylight he has,
Ever since he was a lad.

His favourite film is *Ghost,*
With that bloke Patrick Swayzee,
But his favourite cartoon has to be
The Adventures Of Dolly Daisy.

His favourite drinks are spirits and booze,
He really likes his wine.
Once when he was drunk, his mates shaved off his eyebrows
And hung him on the washing line.

His problem is his singing.
He sings so flat we're reduced to tears.
Even after just one note
We have to cover our ears.

He's a lot like a human being,
He doesn't walk round wearing a sheet.
Everyone sees him as a friend,
That's the ghost who lives up my street.

Alex Masshedar (11)
Shotton Hall Comprehensive School

STARTING THE COMPREHENSIVE

In September I started a new school,
It turned out to be rather cool,
The bell goes ring at half-past eight,
And you've got to try not to be late,
Some lessons are good some lessons are bad,
The teachers are either happy or mad,
The school dinners are really good,
But some people say they taste like mud,
I'm in loads of clubs at school,
Because my new school is really cool!

Graeme Clark (11)
Shotton Hall Comprehensive School

THE MANSION

There was a mansion
Stood on a hill
It was creepy and dark
Not to mention very still

The guys who made it were thick
It was made out of wood
Not brick

Well these guys planted a tree
It grew so big it tumbled
Yes it fell on the mansion with a wham!
And made the mansion crumble
And that was the end of it.

Michael Laws (11)
Shotton Hall Comprehensive School

THE FIRST DAY AT COMP

In 1997,
When I was eleven,
The air felt breezy,
And I felt queasy.

I was worried of bullies,
It was hard to be bold,
I reminded myself of rumours,
That I had been told.

I called for my friends,
They were just fine,
Was I round the bend,
Was I off my mind?

Then at school,
I felt excited,
I went all fuzzy,
And delighted.

Even though bodies
Loomed past my height,
I felt I was cured,
Cured from my fright.

When the day was over,
I was relieved,
It wasn't how
I had believed.

Tracy Dodds (11)
Shotton Hall Comprehensive School

ENVIRONMENTAL DISASTERS!

Sea
I made up this rhyme when I was standing here,
It's all about the sea when it used to be clear,
Dolphins would swim and have a good time,
And now they're all covered in slime.
Loads of whales sang their whale-type song,
And now they're all practically gone.
Humans should know from their past mistakes,
Not to pollute rivers and lakes.

Forest
Cutting down trees is wrong and bad,
If you cut down a tree I'd say you're quite mad.
Trees provide homes for birds and bugs,
Trees provide food for monkeys and slugs.
The shout of 'Timber' makes me think,
Many animals could become extinct.
Even though trees provide wood,
Cutting down trees still isn't good.

City
Car fumes and chimney smoke,
All this pollution makes me choke.
Litter dumped all over the place,
There's even litter in outer space.
All the trees begin to die,
Many birds no longer fly.
We should begin to clear up our mess,
And then all the creatures could safely rest.

Barry Carney (11)
Shotton Hall Comprehensive School

THE BLITZ

The sirens wailed on and on,
down to the shelter,
that's where we'd gone.
We could hear the crumbling,
of buildings that fall,
the screams of children,
'Mum' they call.

The shelter was cold,
I shivered with fear,
and I wondered to myself,
would I ever get out of here.
I might be gone,
I might be dead,
would I soon be lying
in a hospital bed?

When the sirens finally stopped,
out of the shelter we gleefully hopped.
Our house was still standing,
but as I glanced next door,
their house was crackling,
as it fell to the floor.

Another one gone,
another one down,
would ours be next,
to fall to the ground?

Kelly Love (12)
Shotton Hall Comprehensive School

THE ASTRONAUT

The astronaut is glistening white,
like a snowflake falling delicately.

He is a humming bird floating,
like a raft on a motionless river.

That astronaut is the large red spot,
swirling on Jupiter's surface.

He is a tennis ball smacked off a racket,
speeding so fast through the air.

He is all kinds of food as he orbits the earth,
circling different countries.

He is the darting stream,
moving so swift and fast.

The astronaut is like a giant hand,
reaching into space as far as he can.

That astronaut is like a giant shoe,
'One small step for man, one giant leap for mankind'.

Daniel Donbauand (12)
Shotton Hall Comprehensive School

BUMP IN THE NIGHT

Bump in the night what did you hear?
Is it a witch at the rear?
May be a ghost coming near
It must be something, will it appear?
Is it old or is it new?
What do you think will happen to you?

Look under the bed quiet as night
Will it be dead, will you see light?
In the cupboard what can you see?
Spiders and cobwebs next to your knee.
You look all over nothing you find
Till you realise it's all in your mind.

Stephanie Bailey (11)
Shotton Hall Comprehensive School

THE SEASONS

At the end of spring,
Summer will begin.
The butterflies flutter and bees buzz,
The days become hot the sun is out a lot.
In September autumn starts,
The leaves begin to fall to the ground,
They fall without making a sound.
The days become short,
The nights become long,
The church bells ring ding, dang, dong.
Winter's here,
A time to cheer,
Because Christmastime is very near.
But there is fog, the rain, the snow and ice,
This awful weather is not nice.
Spring is back,
With nice warm days,
The seasons.

Bethany Ainsley (11)
Shotton Hall Comprehensive School

SPECK IN THE SKY

Speck in the sky
It gets bigger and bigger through the telescope's eye
Coming in fast
Whose could it be?
Excitement is growing
Fanciers all look to the sky
Coming through wind
Coming through rain
It looks like it's flown all day
Wings flying
Chest heaving
It's coming to us
Could it be ours?
It looks this way
It comes this way
It's right above us now
The old blue hen has landed
The pigeon who won the race.

Andrew Alexander (11)
Shotton Hall Comprehensive School

IN THE STILL OF THE NIGHT

As you hear the wolves howling,
In the still of the night,
You may start to tremble,
You may get a fright.

In the mid of the night,
A wood will appear,
Whenever I watch,
It fills me with fear.

My friend was curious,
He wanted a look,
But paid the price,
For the risk he took.

So when you hear the wolves howling,
In the still of the night,
Just turn and start running,
You'll know you've done right.

Matthew Foxton (11)
Shotton Hall Comprehensive School

How Bizarre

How bizarre
          It really is quite weird
How bizarre
          I grew a beard
How bizarre
          It really is quite scary
How bizarre
          It's getting hairy
How bizarre
          I'm getting quite old
How bizarre
          I'm getting quite bold
How bizarre
          It's getting quite serious
How bizarre
          It's really mysterious
How bizarre
          A hundred am I
How bizarre
          Some day I'll die.

Ian Bell (11)
Shotton Hall Comprehensive School

EPITAPH TO A PIRATE

Here lies the body of Thomas Jones
A pirate to the end
He met his death with Billy Bones
Who drove him round the bend.

He spent his days finding treasure
He spent his nights with crones
A tot of rum three fingers measure
To warm his aching bones.

Beware when boarding a pirate ship
Set sail for where X marks the spot
The treasure he found in a sandy dip
Where Billy Bones guarded the lot.

But now poor Thomas is dead and gone
His ghost walks the plank
And still lives on
With a cry that chills the blood.

Remember Billy Bones will drive you mad
So take along his cheese
And then you will live to a ripe old age
And sail the seven seas.

Laura Laws (11)
Shotton Hall Comprehensive School

THE ELEPHANT

I saw an elephant today,
When he came out from the cupboard
Out to play.

I saw him raise his long great tail,
He sucked with his trunk
And made a shimmering wail.

He sucked up dirt, dust and debris,
He stopped and turned
To look at me.

His face was white so I saw,
Then at the curtains
He began to gnaw.

I saw an elephant today,
When he went home to the cupboard
Home to stay . . .

Jonathan McNay (11)
Shotton Hall Comprehensive School

THE FOUR SEASONS

Our year is four seasons
Winter, spring, summer and autumn.

Winter is so cold and bright.
The snow, the wind, the sleet and the ice.
The snow is white and the stars are so bright.
Then there's the wind so cold, it freezes your toes.

Spring is when the snow melts
And the wind calms down.
The new shoots of flowers, trees and grass all grow now.
Spring has melted the snow at last.

Summer is when the flowers are in bloom.
Their smell is like perfume.
Then colours are so rainbow bright.
Our grass is green, the sun is hot and bright.

Autumn is when trees' leaves dry and die.
The colours they turn are red, gold and brown.
The sun is not so hot.
Winter is just around the corner.

Charlene Price (11)
Shotton Hall Comprehensive School

MY WINTER

Winter, winter my favourite time of year
Sitting in the snow feeling Urrr!
Making a snowman putting on his hat
When I made his face I said goodbye to the cat.
It started to snow, it got really cold
I got frostbite
It was quite a *fright!*
I had some hot chocolate sitting by the fire
There was a film on TV that I really admire.
The snow is melting
I did not want it to go
But I had to go with the flow.
It was coming out of winter
Coming into spring
But it was still winter for me.
It's my birthday today
I blew out candles
And got some sandals
But I can't wear them, I'm upset
Because it's not summer yet.

Lyndsey Todd (11)
Shotton Hall Comprehensive School

HOLIDAYS

Screech went the tyres,
 Bang went the brakes
  My father drove us into the lakes.
  Spit went the wires,
   And *arghh* went me,
    I've crunched up my biscuit,
     And spilt all my tea.

Ann Marie Burke (12)
Wolsingham Comprehensive School

WHAT A SAVE BY THAT KEEPER

What a great save by that keeper
That keeper saves the lot,
Curled shots, chipped shots,
Dipped shots,
That keeper saves the lot.

What a save by that keeper
That keeper saves the lot,
He's good as Seaman, Schmeichel and Shay Given
Put together, because that keeper saves the lot.

What a save by that keeper
That keeper saves the lot,
It does not matter where, how or who takes the shot,
Because that keeper saves the lot.

Jonathan Binks (12)
Wolsingham Comprehensive School

THE DOLPHIN

The dashing, diving dolphin,
A jumping sparkling silhouette,
Against the setting sun along the horizon,
A sleek intelligent creature.

A kind, enchanting animal,
Travelling gracefully through the mysterious sea.
An acrobatic mammal,
Caught to do tricks and performances.

Moving swiftly,
Swimming in large groups,
Communicating quickly with whistles and clicks,
Warning each other of the dangers of horrifying enemies.

Disappearing underwater and leaping out just seconds later,
With the glittering water on its silvery body.
Hunting rapidly, with its alert, sharp mind,
The courageous, dashing, diving dolphin.

Gabriella White (12)
Wolsingham Comprehensive School

SPELLBOUND

My neighbour is a witch,
At night I see her on her broom.
'Mum our neighbour's a witch,'
'Go to bed and stay there.'
Out my window I spy,
She's got a black cat,
Also a cauldron.
'Mum our neighbour's a witch,'
'Get out and stay out,'
I spy in her house,
She's having a bath with a crocodile,
After all this I have to say
'Mum our neighbour's a witch.'

Shea Scott (12)
Wolsingham Comprehensive School

AN EAR FOR THE HOMELESS

Alone and hurt, scared and cold,
Why must they endure this unfair hold?
We take things for granted,
Our lives enchanted.
A cup of hot tea,
To them what would it be?
A relief from the streets,
Not treated like cheats!

They too deserve a chance,
To join in with the dance.
Be like us,
Feel like us,
One of us.
Don't jump to a conclusion,
It's often just confusion.
It's not about colour or state,
It's not them we should hate,
But the people who judge,
Who decide to bear a grudge,
Because they themselves have a home,
While the poorest have no choice but to roam.

It's the same though with blacks,
So many racist attacks
And murders because of skin.
Racism is the sin!
This earth is not perfect,
Many lives have been wrecked,
Because of words, abuse and lies.
Every week someone dies!

Life is unfair,
But some people care.
We can't change this world, but we can do our best
To put our beliefs and views to the test.
Give every person their chance to fit in
And throw your hatefulness in the bin!

Sophie Douglas (13)
Wolsingham Comprehensive School

JAGUAR

Jaguar,
As big and as powerful,
As a jet engine,
As beautiful as a model.

Chased and trapped,
Hunted and caught,
Tortured and killed,
Dead forever.

Jaguar rug and carry case,
Clothes and hats,
Food and medicine,
The jaguar extinct.

Small feeble groups,
Try to help,
While big companies sit back and
Laugh.

Nick Grayson (13)
Wolsingham Comprehensive School

Football

If only I could,
I wish I could,
To play all day
That's all I ask.

If only I could,
I wish I could,
It's any man's dream
To play all day.

If only I could,
I wish I could,
Just to play from
Dawn till dusk.

Jonathan Elliott (12)
Wolsingham Comprehensive School

My House

I love my house,
My house is old,
Old not bold.
When it was sold to us
It was a crate,
Everything was bashed,
The windows were smashed,
And then we fixed it all.
The people thought it was cool,
I love my house.

Louis Tristram (12)
Wolsingham Comprehensive School

My Mischievous Kitten

A little tabby kitten so soft and gay,
Like a fluffy ball or it looks that way.
Purring like a steam train,
Running down a lane.

Pouncing on an innocent mouse,
Bringing it back into the house.
Looking so pleased she gleams,
Until someone screams!

In circles she runs chasing her tail,
As people look they laugh and wail.
She chases other cats,
And nibbles at all the hats.

When she is tired she curls up in a ball,
On the sunny window sill in the hall.
If she's hungry she cries and cries,
Until someone gets up to feed her and sighs.

She's the funniest little kitten you ever saw,
And if you saw her you would want her to play some more.
She lies on your bed and licks your toes,
Just to show she loves you loads.

And her name is Smudge!

Caroline West (12)
Wolsingham Comprehensive School

Elevator

Elevator going
Up
Up
Up,
As it goes faster
Up it goes
But if feels so smooth
Because nobody knows
That we're
Getting nearer to the top
Is it never going to stop
But as it slows down
We're reaching the end of the ride
So a few more people get in
And I have to move
To the side.

Daniel Evans (12)
Wolsingham Comprehensive School

The Goldfish

I'm a little goldfish as happy as can be,
I swim around all day and night,
And wow I'm very light.
I have a little friend,
Who's ill but on the mend.
Her name is Mary,
And she's my little fairy.
I want to stay here,
Where the water is so clear.

Jill Nattrass (12)
Wolsingham Comprehensive School

SHIPS

Plunging across
The foaming sea,
The ship is
A galloping horse,
Leaving behind
A long flowing tail,
With billowing sails
Like a white flying mane.

Pounding across
The rolling sea,
The ship is
A powerful bear,
Forcing its way
Through the breaking waves,
Like the grizzly
Pushing trees to the ground.

Forcing its way
Through the stormy night,
The ship is
A hungry lion,
Stalking its prey
Hour after hour.
Through the vast ocean
Of Savanna

Emma Coxon (12)
Wolsingham Comprehensive School

BLACK CAT

So black and sleek,
Creeping,
Slyly following
No one but himself.

At the slightest noise,
His ears are
Pricking,
Wondering if anyone's there.

His silky black coat
Disguised in the night sky,
Green eyes
Give you a fright.

Perched on the end
Of a broomstick,
Balanced
Nearly falling round every bend.

The witch's loyal lieutenant,
Ever present, graceful, swift,
Familiar,
Elegant, lucky for some.

Bennath Evea (12)
Wolsingham Comprehensive School

PEOPLE

People going places
Busy rushing there
People moving

People at work
Building, typing and phoning
Hard

People at home
Relaxing and enjoying
Rest

People playing
Tennis, hockey and rugby
While having fun.

Michael Stott (12)
Wolsingham Comprehensive School

LIFE

Life is something you cannot explain,
It comes,
And sadly it goes again.
Some lives are happy,
Some lives are sad,
And some lives are just another day of pain.

Life for some is something they don't want,
Or maybe they just can't have.
Some lives are lived in dismay
And fear,
Because the end might be very near.

Why should lives be lived this way?
Lives should be blissful,
Not sad and despaired.
I wonder what some people
Would give,
Just for the life
They will never get to live.

Alice Cleasby (12)
Wolsingham Comprehensive School

In The Corner Of The Field

In the corner of the field,
There's something moving
By the tree in the sunlight,
By the trickling water in the field.

Should we go near?
Should we stay here?
What is it?
I don't know.

It's a dog playing with a stick.
He goes to the water
To take a drink,
Then he has a swim
Round and round in circles.

He goes back to the tree,
He goes and lies down,
He curls up in a ball,
Then he goes to sleep.

Joanne de Muschamp (12)
Wolsingham Comprehensive School

What Are You Doing?

What are you doing when you use CFCs?
What are you doing when you pollute the seas?
What are you doing when you chop down great big trees?
All these things mankind are doing,
Just think to yourself,
What am I doing?

Adam Crampsie (12)
Wolsingham Comprehensive School

CAT!

Sleek,
He walks through the night,
Silent,
He prowls.

Like two stars,
His eyes glow,
Glistening,
In the blackness.

Smelling the air,
Sensing his victim,
Listening,
He roams.

He walks alone,
Independent,
So silent,
He creeps!

Tabitha Willis (12)
Wolsingham Comprehensive School

MY BOAT POEM

There once was a boat
But it just wouldn't float
They tried and tried
But they were still denied
So they had one last go
And *wo ho ho*
It sailed the ocean wide.

Daniel Jackson (13)
Wolsingham Comprehensive School

WORLD

From crowded city streets
To the vast and open emptiness
Of the wide and deep blue sea.
From the erupting of volcanoes
And the rumbling of earthquakes,
To the calm and tranquillity
Of tropical coral islands.

All kinds of life, from
Whales spouting and trout leaping,
To monkeys climbing and flies buzzing.
All these things and many more
Fit into our wonderful world.

Rosemary Menes (13)
Wolsingham Comprehensive School

SPACE!

I've always wanted to go out to space,
Feel the stars touch my face,
See the planets before my eyes,
Sit on the moon and watch the sun rise.

I've always wanted to go out to space,
And have a laugh with a few mates,
Watch the rockets fly past my face,
I never want to go home from *space!*

Sarah Donaldson (12)
Wolsingham Comprehensive School

NOBODY NOTICES

Nobody notices the man in the alleyway
Going through sadness and pain every day
His hair is tatty, never combed
He is a poor unfortunate that needs to be homed

His clothes are dirty and old and torn
Every day the same clothes are worn
Why don't people notice him? Why don't they care?
They all see him, they all know he's there

Why do people walk on by?
Just like snobs their noses up to the sky
If they could only spare him some food
But they don't care they're just cruel and rude

When I see him it makes me cry
Amongst the rubbish is where he does lie
He lives his life hiding in sorrow
You never know, his luck could change tomorrow

But until then he'll live in fear
Jumping at the sound of everything near
It just isn't fair how he has to live like this
Having nobody to love or to kiss

On his own he has to stay
Sadly his troubles look anything but far away
So when you see him lying there
Give him some food, just to show you care.

Jamie Allinson (12)
Wolsingham Comprehensive School

DANDELION

On the lonely road that winds,
My thin green body stands,
And next to me are grassy strands,
Twisting round my body like grabbing hands.

My yellow hair looks like a lion's mane,
I am wild, not tame.
The car engine gasses blow in my face,
It makes me limp, and sets my heart at a fast pace.

Most people call me a weed,
And they hate my time-telling seed.
My babies are scattered all around,
Their fluffy white bodies hitting the ground.

Catriona Maddocks (12)
Wolsingham Comprehensive School

THE OWL

With bright eyes to see in the night,
He spreads his wings and takes flight.
Slowly gliding through the air,
He sees a mouse, he doesn't care
About the family of the mouse.
In the corner of the shed you hear them shout,
'No, no, not Dad.'
If the owl went they would be glad.

But no such luck the mouse can find,
He hears a noise and looks behind.
There behind him is the owl,
Keeping slowly on the prowl.
The owl swoops, and in a flash
There is a stillness in the grass.

Lucy Kilgariff (12)
Wolsingham Comprehensive School

SPIDER

The dark scary spider creeps,
Slowly and silently up the wall.
Sinuously weaving its silk white web
Not once does he ever fall.

Like an acrobat swinging on silken strands,
The spider captures a struggling fly
And wraps it in its coiled threads,
Then lethally injects to make it die.

It twists and turns while slurping blood.
Nothing pleases this killer more,
Than a graveyard full of tattered wings,
A web of flies' guts and gore.

I imagine spiders creeping up on me,
Praying that I won't die.
I hate to think how I would feel,
I'm glad I'm not a fly.

Laurie Shepherd (12)
Wolsingham Comprehensive School

SPIDERS!

I have a fear of spiders,
Do you have a fear of them too?
They creep up your arm, then down your back,
And make me scream ooh!

Some are quite small and colourful,
And others are big and black.
Many have hairy legs and big eyes,
I call those ones Jack.

Their webs seem to stick to your face,
And some seem to glisten in the rain.
It's quite amazing watching them,
They must be clever and have a big brain.

Ashleigh Findeisen (11)
Wolsingham Comprehensive School